"Death never happens no matter what anyone tells you. There is only life . . . in all its iterations. I was lucky to share that with Kelly Sullivan Walden after her near-death experience. Once we know that life doesn't end when the body does, we can get on with the business of living with more freedom and joy. That's what Kelly talks about in this book—she gives us the steps and tools to transform our tragic into magic . . . one metaphorical or literal lightning strike at a time!"

DANNION BRINKLEY, *New York Times* bestselling author of *Saved by the Light*

"*A Crisis Is a Terrible Thing to Waste* reveals how the darkest traumas and misfortunes of our private histories can be transformed into treasure in the form of deeper purpose. In this brave and innovative book, Kelly Sullivan Walden takes the mystery out of such alchemy by systematically revealing, through personal stories and her breakthrough 4-step method, how to face and embrace our nightmares (both waking and sleeping) in order to transmute them into fuel for creating the life of our dreams. This empowering book provides the gift of clarity—the means through which to excavate the mud of our pasts and uncover glimmers of our unique purpose for being alive."

ASPEN MATIS, bestselling author of *Girl in the Woods*
and *Your Blue Is Not My Blue*

"We all face adversities, challenges, and many face crises that leave them paralyzed. But what if in these times the gold is hidden under the mud? Kelly ignites us with practical tools and soulful wisdom to find our inner magician to free us from our personal cage and give us wings to believe that indeed we are the alchemist of our own life! And how grand is that?! Read the treasures of this book and find your magic tools."

AGAPI STASSINOPOULOS, bestselling author of *Speaking with Spirit*

"As Carl Jung once said, 'One does not become enlightened by imagining figures of light, but by making the darkness conscious.' In Kelly Sullivan Walden's latest book, *A Crisis Is a Terrible Thing to Waste*, she does just that. She not only reveals her own shadowy stories and shares how she mined the gold from them, but she leaves a trail of breadcrumbs behind, along with a system to help us take our disempowered stories and transform them into the launching pad for our greatest compassion and contribution to humanity. And she does all this with the ability to belly-laugh at the dark, making sure it has no choice but to turn into light."

CYNDI DALE, bestselling and award-winning author of *The Subtle Body*

"For many of us, one of the muddiest areas of our lives is in the realm of our intimate relationships. If we want to attract and sustain the soulmate relationship of our dreams, we need to stop glossing over our heartbreaks. Instead, we need to read Kelly Sullivan Walden's latest book, *A Crisis Is a Terrible Thing to Waste*, to help us shine a bright light on our crippling love-life woes to transform them into WOWs—and thus, become magnetic to the love we desire and deserve."

ARIELLE FORD, bestselling author of *The Soulmate Secret*

"Never in history (most certainly not in my history) has the bleep hit the fan more than it has lately. I am deeply aware of the fact that life can make us either bitter or better. This is why I love Kelly Sullivan Walden's latest book, *A Crisis Is a Terrible Thing to Waste*. It helps us get down to the nitty gritty, to not just tolerate but celebrate the things in life that tip us upside down and shake us by the ankles. With Kelly's OGLE process, you'll learn how to quickly transform your tragic into magic."

BETSY CHASSE, award-winning coproducer/director
of *What the Bleep Do We Know*

"When it appears like things are falling apart, a new world is trying to emerge—a world of higher values and vision. A world that works for the highest good of all. But it can't happen apart from us. We each need to participate in this emergence by becoming the change we want to see in the world (personally, professionally, and globally). For this reason, I'm so excited about my friend Kelly Sullivan Walden's new book, *A Crisis Is a Terrible Thing to Waste*. She gets into the nitty-gritty in her simple 4-step formula to teach us all how to transform our most difficult moments into a springboard into our greatest emergence."

DEREK RYDALL, bestselling author of *Emergence*

"Having our dream life—a life where our greatest desires come to pass—is our birthright. But it doesn't materialize without us learning some hard lessons along the way. I prefer the easy way—don't get me wrong—but I'm grateful for my missteps and challenges because they've deepened me and given me access to valuable aspects of my inner wisdom that I never would've discovered otherwise. To help us flip the tragic into magic, I recommend the radically simple but profound 4-step process Kelly Sullivan Walden writes about in her book *A Crisis Is a Terrible Thing to Waste*."

CHRISTY WHITMAN, *New York Times* bestselling author

"I hope your life is filled with grace, ease, and phenomenal prosperity. However, if you should encounter a bump in the road or any type of difficulty, my wish for you is that you learn how to see that life is never happening to you but for you. This is one of the reasons why I love Kelly Sullivan Walden's book *A Crisis Is a Terrible Thing to Waste*. It teaches us an enlightened perspective on how to perceive our tribulations and transform them into jubilation. The medicine in her 4-step OGLE process is truly life changing. I hope this book impacts you at least half as much as it has me!"

MARIE DIAMOND, bestselling author and star of *The Secret*

"Could there be a more important time in our lives to learn the energy healing tools to pull ourselves out of the mud than now? I don't think so. In fact, to become able to transform our tragic moments into magic moments (as quickly and thoroughly as possible) is the name of the game. This is why I wholeheartedly recommend Kelly Sullivan Walden's latest book, *A Crisis Is a Terrible Thing to Waste*. This book is for anyone who wants to make the most at their difficulties to become the best version of themselves—to be able to pay it forward and make a difference on this planet."

LISA CAMPION, bestselling author of
The Art of Psychic Reiki and Energy Healing for Empaths

"From one who is no stranger to the mud, phenomenal Kelly and her amazing book is the perfect inspiration to remind us to STOP wasting our funky moments—they are so deliciously (albeit intensely) rife with learning, growing . . . and let's face it, Sacred Exfoliation! I highly recommend it as a way to ensure the transformation of your tragic into your magic."

ALLANA PRATT, author of *From Heartbreak to HeartMates*

"Everyone in my world knows that I am a huge proponent of falling in love with our shadows. My dear friend Kelly Sullivan Walden has written a book of her own personal shadows and her process of not just tolerating them but celebrating them. When I think of the world I want to live in, it's one where we all stop glossing over or ignoring our difficulties and most painful memories, but one where we love them so much they become our access point to truly making a difference in other people's lives and creating great meaning in our own."

JO-E SUTTON, author of the upcoming book *Falling in Love with Your Shadows*

A *Crisis* Is a Terrible Thing to Waste

A *Crisis* Is a Terrible Thing to Waste

THE ART OF TRANSFORMING THE TRAGIC INTO MAGIC

KELLY SULLIVAN WALDEN

BEYOND WORDS
Portland, Oregon

BEYOND WORDS

1750 S.W. Skyline Blvd., Suite 20
Portland, Oregon 97221-2543
503-531-8700 / 503-531-8773 fax
www.beyondword.com

First Beyond Words paperback edition January 2023

BEYOND WORDS PUBLISHING and colophon are registered trademarks of
Beyond Words Publishing. Beyond Words is an imprint of Simon & Schuster, Inc.

For more information about special discounts for bulk purchases, please contact
Beyond Words Special Sales at 503-531-8700 or specialsales@beyondword.com.
Managing editor: Lindsay Easterbrooks-Brown

Managing editor: Lindsay Easterbrooks-Brown
Editor: Bailey Potter
Copyeditor: Kristin Thiel
Proofreader: Ashley Van Winkle
Design: Sara E. Blum
Composition: William H. Brunson Typography Services

Manufactured in the United States of America

10 9 8 7 6 5 4 3 2 1

Library of Congress Cataloging-in-Publication Data:

Names: Walden, Kelly Sullivan, author.
Title: A crisis is a terrible thing to waste : the art of transforming the
   tragic into magic / Kelly Sullivan Walden.
Description: First Beyond Words paperback edition. | Portland, Oregon :
   Beyond Words, 2023.
Identifiers: LCCN 2022037500 (print) | LCCN 2022037501 (ebook) | ISBN
   9781582708812 (paperback) | ISBN 9781582708829 (ebook)
Subjects: LCSH: Self-actualization (Psychology) | Dreams—Therapeutic use.
   | Mental healing.
Classification: LCC BF637.S4 W343 2023 (print) | LCC BF637.S4 (ebook) |
   DDC 158.1—dc23/eng/20221026
LC record available at https://lccn.loc.gov/2022037500
LC ebook record available at https://lccn.loc.gov/2022037501

The corporate mission of Beyond Words Publishing, Inc.: *Inspire to Integrity*

Dedication

To those who've been to hell and back more times than you can count, and are still in the trenches, may this book help you alchemize your drama into the phenomena of your unique pearls of wisdom. May these stories inspire you to remember that the worst things can become the best things, when you lift your gaze from the tragic and develop eyes to behold the magic that is always here.

A percentage of proceeds from this book benefits the Claire's Place Foundation.[1]

A human being is essentially a spirit-eye.
Whatever you really see, you are that.

RUMI

Contents

Contents

Foreword

Kelly Sullivan Walden's way of transforming tragic to magic is a powerful practice, especially these days when we are facing such difficult times and hearing heartbreaking news on a daily basis. To live in a state of victimhood (a natural response to tragedy) can have the effect of a dam impeding the flow of joy in our lives. In order to break the dam, we need the recognition of the deeper nature of the tragedy (to initiate us to our purpose and resilience) and the courage to face the challenges they present. As Kelly points out in *A Crisis Is a Terrible Thing to Waste*, the key is to look beneath the surface to discover the inspiration for a new, artful, life-affirming creation—a tip I personally put to practice while working through my own crisis, so it wouldn't leave its thick residue in my mind.

It might seem strange, but I consider my greatest attribute as being an ogler. It's my style—without necessarily meaning to—to provoke my students out of their comfort zones; out of trying to get it right; out of being good and commonplace. I often flip my students' paintings upside down while they're mid brushstroke, to show them a more creative and sometimes even absurd way of perceiving art, and thus, life. To be an ogler of the artistic or transformational variety is one and the same. We must develop the eyes to see beyond the surface if we're to have a life of inspiration. Why else did we bother incarnating?

—Rassouli, founder of the FusionArt movement
and bestselling author of *Sufi Wisdom Oracle*

Preface

PERSEPHONE, PHONE HOME

It is by going down into the abyss that we recover the treasures of life. Where you stumble, there lies your treasure.

JOSEPH CAMPBELL

The goddess Persephone, according to myth, was the epitome of innocence and all things lovely. One day, while frolicking through the meadow chasing butterflies and cartwheeling amid the wildflowers, she was seized by the captivating aroma of the narcissus. As the prepubescent maiden beheld the flower's snow-white petals, she breathed in the mysterious scent and caught her first whiff of self-awareness. To document the moment, she whipped out her phone, feeling inexplicably compelled to pose for her first selfie.

At this exact time, Hades, god of the underworld, who'd been stalking Persephone like an obsessed paparazzo, seized the window of opportunity caused by the flower's narcotic roofie-esque effect on the young goddess. The dark king reached his scaly hand from his shadowy lair and clutched Persephone's ankle. Before she could reach for her pepper spray or utter a single "OMG," she was abducted from the life she'd known and became a missing person.

Persephone kicked, screamed, and prayed to be rescued by her helicopter parent, Demeter, goddess of the harvest. But the earth swallowed her wailing, and her mother could not hear her cries.

Exhausted, eventually Persephone realized she could not outrun or outsmart her captor. Surrendering to Stockholm syndrome, she relented to becoming Hades's bride, and thus queen of the underworld. To mark the occasion, she got a tattoo, dyed her dress black, and painted her nails goth blue. A sudden student of the dark arts, she learned to use the *Thoth Crowley Taro*t to understand the past, the Ouija board to forecast the future, and alchemy to transform dense matter into gold.

Six months later, just as Persephone was finding the bright side of perpetual darkness, Zeus sent Apollo on his winged chariot to save her and the earth due to Demeter having turned the world to ice from the heartbreak of her daughter's dissappearance. Before Persephone was escorted back to the world above, clever Hades offered her a few parting gifts: six pomegranate seeds, one for each month she'd been with him.

Famished after not having eaten since she'd been there, she gobbled them up. As she licked the crimson, blood-like juice from the back of her hand, she flipped Hades the finger and wished him a not-so-fond adieu.

Apparently, everyone but Persephone read the memo clearly stating never to eat food in the underworld. Because she consumed this Hadean snack, she'd have to return to Hades for six months of every year.

Once Persephone arrived back upon the soil of upper earth, reunited with her mother, the sun peeked from behind the frosty clouds, and life on earth resumed: birds chirped, butterflies fluttered, and humans boasted on social media about how the offerings they made to the gods contributed to the rescue of their beloved Persephone.

While the world celebrated, Persephone was standoffish and discombobulated. No longer the virginal girl and no longer queen of shadows, she wondered, "Who am I? Will the real Persephone please stand up?"

In time, Persephone did stand up as she came to see that because of what she'd endured, she'd earned dual citizenship, being granted access to the realms of darkness and light. With the ability to live boldly, powerfully, and fearlessly in both worlds, she became heralded as a healer/alchemist/dreamer/goddess, a bridge being, and thus a force to be reckoned with.

No matter how charmed our lives may be, we all take our tour of duty in the Hadean realm via a dark night of the soul (or several of them). It's not a matter of *if*, but *when*.

Because of my unexpected sojourns to the dark side and back, having taken in more than my share of pomegranate seeds, I know the terrain. Through this book I'll take you on a journey back and forth, across the alchemy bridge, so maybe you, like Persephone and me, will not only unpack the precious wisdom you've earned and learned from your dark nights, but milk them for all they're worth.

Introduction

*One does not become enlightened by imagining figures
of light, but by making the darkness conscious.*

CARL JUNG

NOTE ABOUT THIS BOOK'S TITLE

I'd like to say I dreamed up the title of this book, *A Crisis Is a Terrible Thing to Waste*, but I'd be lying. I can't remember exactly where I first heard the phrase, but when I did, it rang such a deep chord in me, it quickly became one of my favorite slogans. Since writing this book, I've become aware of Paul Romer's use of the phrase, as well as Rahm Emanuel's subsequent popularization of it.[2]

In spite of these references, this book has nothing to do with politics or economics. It relates to transformation of the very personal, individual—mind, body, and spirit—variety. This strangely may be the most potent way to affect political and economic change.

Additionally, the notion of *A Crisis Is a Terrible Thing to Waste* also relates to a theory that's become well-known in recent years: post-traumatic growth (PTG). You are, no doubt, familiar with Post-Traumatic Stress Disorder (PTSD) but what you might not be as familiar with is the work of Richard Tedeschi, PhD, and Lawrence Calhoun, PhD, that explains the phenomena of extreme transformation that can follow a traumatic event, if we allow it. According to this theory, 50 percent of people who endure an adverse circumstance see radically positive growth afterward.[3]

With all this in mind, I hope the title of this book and its contents inspire you to look for and find the gold in the midst of any and all challenges you or your loved ones may face.

DISCLAIMER

I've written these true stories to the best of my memory, which is admittedly imperfect and limited. I have changed some names and identifying characteristics to protect the innocent and not so innocent. Despite the fact that the core of each of these stories is true (including a few that have been previously printed in other publications), some events and people have been amalgamized for literary cohesion.

Also, you should know, I'm not the type to "wear my pain on my sleeve," which is why, in all my previous books, I've mostly written from a place of authority, as a dream expert. I'm proud of those books, don't get me wrong. However, I've recently discovered that people seem to learn more from me when I let them in on my more vulnerable "tragic to magic" stories than when I just skip straight to the "magic." It seems the learning is not only more relatable but more empowering when I reveal how I nearly drowned in the mud of victimhood (over and over and over) and eventually found my way to the light. In other words, if you're familiar with my work, you'll notice this book is different from the others.

This collection of essays relates true stories from my life, and they all feature some measure of small or large crises—shining a light on my flaws, insecurities, and embarrassing and naïve moments. I present them here on a messy platter for you to learn from, relate to, or judge. Be careful of judging, however, as when we judge someone else, we judge ourselves.

None of us discover true wisdom without going through the muck. In this book, I highlight my journey to inspire you, so next time you fall, you'll remember to look for the message in the mess, and the magic amid the tragic. After all, what you look for, you find.

MY NITTY, GRITTY, SHITTY LIST

You might be wondering what in God's name am I—a white, fifty-four-year-old woman from a middle-class family in the US living in the twenty-first century—doing writing a book with the word *crisis* in the title? My Irish ancestors, survivors of the potato famine, would scoff in their graves: "Ach! What does our girl know about crisis?"

Ancestry aside, let's pretend you and I are on a first date in a lovely restaurant, seated in a window-side booth, and we just ordered dinner. As we sip floral wine from crystal glasses, you look across the table, past the red rose in the vase and the flickering candle, smiling as you innocently say, "So, tell me about yourself."

I clear my throat, dab the cloth napkin to my lips, take a breath, look you intently in the eye, and reply, "Aw, thanks. I'm happy to. Yeah, there are a few things you should know about me if we're going to have a relationship beyond this date." First, I'll get my nitty, gritty, shitty list out of the way as I reach into my purse and say, "I've prepared a document for such an occasion."

You watch, spellbound, as I unfurl a very long scroll from my purse, clear my throat again, and read aloud:

- While I perused acting in my twenties, I had over one hundred indecent #MeToo-esque propositions.

- One of those led to me becoming a stripper in a bikini bar for a year... and then, I...

  - *was robbed five times*
  - *was physically assaulted and nearly raped four times*
  - *was in three car accidents*
  - *contemplated suicide twice*
  - *was mauled by dogs once*
  - *jumped off a sixty-foot-high cliff and landed ass-first in the water*
  - *bounced checks*
  - *dropped out of college*
  - *shoplifted*
  - *dabbled in eating disorders*

- I used to be irresistibly drawn to dysfunctional relationships where I was...

  - *lied to*
  - *manipulated*
  - *conned*
  - *cheated*
  - *rejected*
  - *stalked*
  - *forced to file restraining orders*
  - *up close and personal with the mafia*

- All this has led me to become . . .

    - *a commitment-phobe with a messianic complex*
    - *an insecure, codependent, workaholic*
    - *in grief over the recent-ish death of over a dozen loved
      ones, including two lifelong best friends, Theresa
      and Gypsy, and most recently, my lapdogs/constant
      companions, Lola and Priya*

- But my biggest heartbreak was the death of a baby I was
  scheduled to adopt . . .

- And, in the time it took me to tell you this, I've had one of the
  fifty hot flashes I'll experience today.

"Now that we've gotten that out of the way . . . I'm going to the
little girls' room. If you're still here when I return, maybe you'll tell
me about you."

I'm happily surprised you're still here when I return, maybe
because you're too stunned by my confession to walk, run, or hide
under the table. But assuming you stayed for another reason, I take
a sip of wine, lean in, and say, "OK, I've shown you mine; now show
me yours. Has your life been a walk in the park or on the wild side?
Has it been confetti-ed with blessings or challenges? Let's meet
beneath the bs of 'fabulous and fine' and get real."

To encourage you to start talking, I add, "By the way, I shared
with you my nitty, gritty, shitty list not to scare you or engender
pity. It was hard for me to share my list with you. In fact, my ego

would prefer to blowtorch it and pretend it doesn't exist, while convincing you I'm perfect and fabulous. Despite my ego, I shared my list with you in the spirit of disclosure, transparency, and authenticity. . . because life is short and whether our relationship lasts just for today or for the long haul, I want it to be as real as possible. I shared this with you because I want to meet you in the truth of our flawed and fractured humanness, and our awe-inspiring luminescence, the both/and, the above/below, the shadow/light, side by side, swirled together, slam dancing in the same mosh pit."

With that mini mic drop, I finally shut up, take a bite of my lasagna, which by now has gone tepid, and allow space for you to tell your story to me. I imagine a choir of angels singing to celebrate that you're sharing your deepest, darkest secrets with me, and because I've finally, thank the Lord, stopped talking.

I'm aware I've not experienced every crisis known to humankind. Not even close, nor would I want to. But in addition to overcoming my own difficulties, over the past twenty-five years, as a certified clinical hypnotherapist, human design analyst, and spiritual counselor—with an emphasis on dreamwork—I've worked with clients who have survived unfathomable hardships. When I added those to my personal list of heartbreaks, I noticed a pattern emerge that reveals the simple formula I articulate here. All this inspired me to write this book with the word *crisis* in the title to share with you why I believe it's a terrible thing to waste . . . and what you can do about it.

危機

The Chinese got it right with their word for *crisis*: the symbol for "danger" and "opportunity." In other words, we each can paint a picture of our life as the victim—"woe is me"—or as victorious: "Wow! There's me! I survived!"

I've come to the point where I now see my proudest accomplishments exist not despite but *because* of my heartbreaks. These hardships broke me open so profoundly, that I (eventually) was able to discover the hidden wisdom and empathy to:

- write eleven books, five oracle decks, and two journals

- earn a doctorate degree in ministerial studies

- be invited to speak at the United Nations

- start a nonprofit organization that inspires thousands of inner-city kids to dream solutions for their personal challenges as well as the UN's goals

- be featured on national television, radio, and magazines

- travel around the world

- meet with and interview some of the world's most inspirational people

- be married to a wonderful man for the last twenty years

- have deep relationships with my family and friends
- live in a beautiful home in the woods I love waking up in every day

In short, I have a life of passion, purpose, and meaning I wouldn't trade with anyone more beautiful, wealthy, famous or thin or with more social media followers. The best things in my life, I know, would not be possible if it weren't for all the unfortunate situations I've lived through. And . . . as full as this book is of my personal dramas, there are more where these came from. Even though I wouldn't want to go through any of them again, I'm grateful for them all. I know it might sound crazy . . . but read on, and you'll learn why.

OGLE

In spite of my nitty, gritty, shitty list and my multiple trips to Hades, you might be surprised to know I'm a mostly happy, peaceful, grateful person. However, no matter what I do to prepare myself for crises (like, say, a pandemic where the world goes into lockdown, and I can't see my family for a year, and people I know and love get sick and die), they always shock me. I know the answer doesn't lie in denial; nor does it lie in excessive wallowing and teeth gnashing. I'm of the opinion that pain is guaranteed—suffering, however, is optional. In other words, I want to milk my challenges for all their worth, as quickly as possible, so I can get back to the business of enjoying my life . . . and I want you to, also!

It is commonly believed that "time heals." But when I was a guest speaker at The Grief Coach Academy a few years ago, I was shocked to hear the founder, Aurora Winter, talk about an article in *Time* magazine that discussed the work of psychologist Doctor Edward

Diener (who did extensive research on the time it takes to recover from debilitating loss). According to that article, "it takes five to eight years for a widow to regain her previous sense of well-being."[4]

Aurora went on to say,

> The cost of suffering from grief is staggering. Joy, health, vitality, relationships, creativity, productivity, clarity, prosperity all suffer. The *Wall Street Journal* reported that the workplace cost of grief is $75 billion per year in the US due to lost productivity, accidents, and absenteeism. Chronic stress from grief can prematurely age your cells by a decade. It can even trigger early death.[5]

However, what I've discovered over my two decades of working with clients (and three decades working on myself), with the right kind of emotional/spiritual/psychological tools, recovery time can be reduced to months, weeks, days, hours, or even minutes.

In the last twenty-five years, I have had the honor, as a hypnotherapist and spiritual coach, to give clients tools to pull themselves out of their quicksand. The OGLE process, if I may toot my own horn, is my best one yet. It's the one I've been looking for my whole life—to quickly turn my and my clients' "tragic into magic."

Allow me to explain.

When I met world-renowned artist Rassouli—with whom I was blessed enough to create the *Dream Oracle* and *Hero's Journey Dream Oracle* decks—he described himself as an ogler of the artistic variety. With his penetrating perspective, he is delighted and enchanted with the most minute details of life around him and does not take beauty at face value.

In the same way Rassouli is an artistic ogler, I invite you to become an ogler of the transformational variety. In fact, one of the best ways to *not* transform a tragic circumstance into magic is to not really look at it and see it for what it is. And one of the best ways to alchemize a crisis—and not waste it—is to truly look at it . . . to OGLE it:

O: What is the Offending behavior and/or situation?

G: What is Good about that offending behavior and/or situation?

L: How am I peering into the Looking Glass (mirror)?

E: How will I allow this situation to Elevate me? What Elevated action will I take?

Let's unpack OGLE, letter by letter.

O: *What is the Offending behavior and/or situation?*

Call to mind a situation where a person . . .

- pissed you off

- hurt your feelings

- let you down

- did exactly the opposite of what you needed, hoped for, assumed, imagined a sane, rational person would do, say, or behave like . . .

This is where you have full permission to feel your feelings. I highly recommend journaling to vent as you rant, rave, and rage. What did this person (or institution or happening) do to you? How did this offensive behavior hurt, scare, upset, devastate, or trigger you? What about this offending behavior bothers you so much? Let it rip. Feel free to blame to your heart's content. There will be plenty of time for self-responsibility in the next steps.

Oh yes, I highly recommend you don't approach the person who offended you until after you've completed the OGLE process. In my experience, it's rare the conversation goes well with the person who hurt my feelings when I'm in the heat of my upset. The possibility of a productive heart-to-heart is usually not possible until we get the bee (or hornet, as the case may be) out of our proverbial bonnet. Of course, there are rare moments in life where reactivity is healthy and useful. However, in my decades of experience, I've discovered that more often than not, it's destructive and can lead to irreparable damage. To address the offending situation directly, with the one who stimulated the upset, in the heat of the fire, requires the skill of a meticulous surgeon. I believe we'll all get there one day. That's, in fact, the goal. But until we achieve this level of mastery, I highly recommend you alchemize your upset via OGLE; then, if appropriate, approach the person who did the offending behavior.

You might be wondering, "What if the person who did the offending behavior was me?"

If you are asking this question, let me congratulate you for the self-awareness to even consider your own culpability. I believe self-OGLE-ing is next to godliness, the ultimate in humility—not humiliation (though it might sometimes feel that way). To admit you misspoke, misstepped, misread, or mishandled a situation—followed by a willingness to learn, grow, and take an elevated action—is the name of the game.

G: *What is Good about that offending behavior and/or situation?*

This is where you look at me like I've lost my whole mind as you rebut indignantly, "Are you insane? There is absolutely NOTHING AT ALL REEDEMABLE, MUCH LESS GOOD, about this horrible, thoughtless, cruel, offensive behavior this person did TO ME."

And I reply, "Yes, I totally understand why you feel that way. And if you want to spend more time in the *O* before you move to the *G*, then be my guest. When you get bored of ranting and raving about how horribly someone did you wrong, and you can't wait to trade in your poopy diapers for a clean pair of big-girl panties or big-boy boxers, then the *G* will be here waiting for you with open arms."

One good thing about their offending behavior is it would only be offensive to you if you didn't have a strong moral value on the opposite end of the spectrum from their behavior. The fact that you are offended is a good thing because it demonstrates you value honesty, integrity, kindness, equity, fill-in-the-blank.

Here's another hint: When all else fails, look beneath their hurtful behavior and notice there is likely a "protective mechanism" at play. Even if you deem the protective mechanism uncalled for, the fact that the person who offended you has self-preservation operating in their psyche means they have a self they feel is worth preserving. Clearly, they've been triggered (otherwise, I imagine their behavior would not have offended you), and it likely comes from some distorted perception, maybe even a PTSD fight/flight/freeze response.

L: *How am I peering into the Looking Glass (mirror)?*

Or: How do I do the same thing? How am I looking in the mirror? Have I ever done this? How do I do this same behavior (or can I imagine how I might if I were in their situation) . . . even if it's just a minuscule speck compared to them?

This is where you get to ride your high horse and say, "Neigh . . . I would never do that! How dare you even assume I would! Off with your head for insinuating something so vile! Don't you know who I am?"

Of course I know who you are. You are me, and I am you. We are all mirror reflections of each other, and kumbaya, hallelujah, and pass the kombucha. The entire human race lives (even if only as a grain of a dust mote) in the entirety of your being. This is where we get the saying "There, but for the grace of God, go I."

E: *How will I allow this situation to Elevate me? What Elevated action will I take?*

In other words, how might this situation be making me a more aware, more compassionate version of myself?

If this is hard to answer, consider the quote widely attributed to Albert Einstein, "The most important question facing humanity is, 'Is the universe a friendly place?'" In other words, your perception of the universe as friendly or hostile will determine the frame you place around all events that take place in your life. If you can perceive that the universe is on your side—that what happens to you is designed to uplift and make you a lighter, brighter, more magnificent you—then it won't be a leap to explore how your circumstance might serve to make you better (not bitter).

If you can answer the question "How will I allow this situation to Elevate me?" (even if you have to imagine you are playing the role of an attorney, arguing the case before a grand jury, looking for evidence of how this situation could be a blessing provoking an improvised version of you to emerge), then you are offi-cially an alchemist.

Did you do it? Did you OGLE your upset?

If you did, bravo! Well done!

If not, do yourself a favor and go back through this process

and give it a shot. To help you, here's an example of how I OGLEd a devastating moment in my life.

THE HIPPY AND THE HYPOCRITE

Years ago, a journalist from my local paper came to my home to interview me for a cover story on the power of dreams. I felt honored to have come so far in my career as a forty-four-year-old dream therapist to warrant the attention of a reporter coming to my house, and I was a nervous wreck. Wanting to make a good impression, before she arrived, I scurried around, tidying the living room, trying to perfectly place the throw blankets on the arms of my chairs so they would look accidentally tossed. I wafted earthy incense and arranged my favorite turquoise scarf around my neck twenty different ways to find the perfect professional yet casual look.

When I heard the knock at the door, I felt ready to face down the entire *60 Minutes* crew. But no! Here was a middle-aged woman with a warm, hippy-chick style that disarmed me immediately. I felt a sisterly vibe as we both nestled on the couch, making small talk and sipping iced teas.

"Are there any topics I should avoid?" my new friend asked, eyes wide over her glass.

"Absolutely not! I'm an open book. You can ask me anything," I quipped, having no idea I'd soon regret saying this.

The conversation flowed easily. About thirty minutes in, she asked, "Why do we have nightmares?"

Ah, one of my favorite topics. I went on a long meander about how nightmares are actually the heroes of our subconscious, helping guide us to healing and wholeness. "There's gold beneath the shadows," I said. "The payoff of doing shadow work with our nightmares is we eventually have nothing to hide or run from, and our lives can become filled with confidence, freedom, and joy."

She nodded and scribbled away. Then she looked up and asked quietly: "Is that how you feel today about your past as a stripper?"

What?

I gripped the arm of the couch, unsure I'd heard her correctly.

Her voice warbled in slow motion: "Do you ever dream about your past as a pole dancer?"

Is this what tasering feels like? I struggled to find my voice. "How... did you know?" I finally asked.

"You shared it, years ago, in a twelve-step recovery meeting."

Yes. I'd been in Al-Anon—to deal with my codependent relationship with alcoholics in my life. Then I dabbled in AA for eight sober years until I discovered I wasn't a true alcoholic. Never mind that "anonymous" is the very heart of those organizations, and anything said in those meetings is supposed to stay inside the meeting. I wasn't interested right then at calling her out on her breach of twelve-step protocol. What I wanted was to get my wind back from this sucker punch. I was a professional, a respected author and expert in a field that heals and uplifts people's minds and spirits. I was not spinning on poles, wearing G-strings from Trashy Lingerie, or taking grocery bags of dollar bills to deposit with smirking bank clerks.

Not anymore.

My breath came back. I gave a wobbly smile to the journalist. "I feel like a hypocrite," I admitted. "I'm promoting living transparently and embracing the shadow, but . . ." I stopped and tried to keep pleading out of my voice. "I'm afraid if my past became public knowledge, it might be the end of the work I do, especially with school kids. I said I was an open book . . . but it turns out I'm not. I have to ask you not to mention my past in this article."

She nodded and asked a few innocuous questions, and the interview hobbled to a close. But I felt no relief when I closed the door after her. I sat back down on the couch, still stunned. Fraud, I thought. Yes, she was the one who did the morally questionable "gotcha." But who was I to talk about openness and embracing nightmares when it was clear I had a backyard dumpster of my own?

I want to be clear about something. Dancing, stripping is a legitimate profession. I don't judge those who choose to make money by taking control of their own bodies and sexuality. But the key word here is *choose*. In my own life, I don't regret stripping off my clothes; I regret stripping myself of my values. I regret giving others agency over my life and letting them decide how to use my body to get what they wanted. I regret believing in others' ideas about me rather than my own abilities. I regret hiding, rationalizing, half-explaining, and lying about what I did for a living back then.

As with any nightmare, the "evil" isn't the monster itself; it's our fear, our hiding and our running from it. My stripping career was brief, but it left a long, long shadow, and as I cleaned up the iced-tea glasses, I knew it was time I discovered the gold beneath it.

Here's how I eventually OGLE'd it:

O: *What is the Offending behavior and/or situation?*

The reporter was being sneaky, trying to expose me in a shaming way.

G: *What is Good about that offending behavior and/or situation?*

Beneath the salaciousness, I perceived her to be on a quest for honesty, truth telling, no bullshit.

L: *How am I peering into the Looking Glass (mirror)?*

I am also intrigued by honesty. Even though the mere thought of being revealed makes me shake and sweat, as I imagine being made to wear a scarlet letter, as I'm stoned by mobs of scorning, judgmental people, I secretly desire to be the open book I purport to be.

E: *How will I allow this situation to Elevate me? What Elevated action will I take?*

I am grateful she called me out in a relatively benign way. This could've been worse. This was my local paper—not *People* magazine. What if this was an invitation for me to up my game and live a more transparent life?

So, I promised myself I would never let that happen again. I decided in the painful clarity of that moment, if anyone is going to expose me, it should be me. And the only way to do that would be to write my own story. So, I did.

I wrote a four-hundred-page memoir titled *Stripped: Dancing with My Demons in the City of Angel*s about my twenty-first year, when I was conned into stripping by a manipulative and oh-so-convincing producer, who lured me in with promises of fortune and fame.

Because of the degree of my shame, I had to take extreme measures to find my way to elevate out of the pit I found myself mired in. I believe if we truly want to transform the tragic into magic, we must call on our secret weapon: creativity. The process of writing *Stripped* turned out to be the best therapy I'd ever done and truly turned my broken soul and heart into art and proved that even the most difficult things we've been through can be alchemized. In fact, every time I talk with someone who's read my story, our conversation pierces the topsoil of normal, polite conversation and suddenly becomes deep, confessional, and soul to soul. I feel lucky (instead of yucky) about my past because it gives me this strange access to meet people in the hidden realm of their most sacred and secret selves.

If you don't believe me about the ability to transform the tragic into magic, check out the work of Victor Frankl, author of the book *Man's Search for Meaning*. Or Eva Mozes Kor, who chronicled her horrific abuse as a twin child surviving Nazi concentration camps in *Surviving the Angel of Death*. Fifty years after her release, she realized she still wasn't free from being haunted daily by her memories. As a true victim, she was struck by the awareness there was nothing she could do to change the past, but she could change the future by shifting her perspective in the present. She tried every other way to free herself, but nothing worked until she discovered the power she possessed to forgive. She created a document of amnesty, forgiving her captors. Not because they deserved it, not because she condoned their behavior, but because she discovered it was the only option she could find to give her a lasting sense of freedom.[6]

There are many victims, including Eva's twin sister, Miriam, who disowned her for her action. But there were many others, in fact, millions of survivors, inspired by her radical act of mercy, who found self-empowerment born from forgiving the unforgivable.

Whether our pain or shame be tiny or monumental, it becomes poison inside us until we turn it into gold. We may not be omnipotent beings who can control the universe, but we do have the power to become alchemists. This ability may not make us impenetrable, but it makes us capable of, on a dime, or in due time, transforming the tragic aspects of our lives into magic.

Amor Fati

Italy

Strangers are friends we haven't met yet.
ANONYMOUS

Have you ever felt the uncontrollable urge to sing Janis Joplin's "Me and Bobby McGee" at the top of your lungs? "Busted flat in Baton Rouge, waiting for a train," when you were waiting for a train?[7]

My husband, Dana, and I were on our last leg of a six-week journey through Spain and Italy, where I'd been leading workshops (which required no extra baggage), but Dana had been recording a flamenco fusion album and shooting a music video, which required a ton of audio- and video-recording equipment. So, along with our backpacks that felt filled with bowling balls and giant-size roller bags stuffed with clothes and whatnots, we schlepped through the Milan train station, sweating, cussing, moaning, and groaning as we climbed up and down stairs, through long tunnels and passageways.

At last, we finally settled on our train that would drop us off in walking distance from our hotel, so we could fly home to Lòs Angeles the next morning. I looked up to see a strange man glaring at me whom my mind registered as the spitting image of Gru from the animated movie *Despicable Me*. With his rounded shoulders, thick neck, long nose, dark circles under his eyes . . . if ever there was the stereotypical villain, here he was.

I shivered as I looked away out the window and tried to distract myself by enjoying the scenery. Just as my adrenaline was calming, a scratchy, barely discernable Italian voice announced what sounded like the name of the station where we should exit . . . but it was way too soon, according to my calculations (which are always to be questioned.)

I flipped my gaze around to read the faded sign outside the window, looked down at my map, back and forth several times, as the door automatically shut before my brain had a chance to compute. I frantically asked the passengers around us, deliberately avoiding eye contact with Gru, in my broken Spanish-ish-Italian-ish hybrid (I felt more confident speaking Spanish, and since Italian is also a romance language, I just blended them, hoping something coherent fell out of my mouth). All my effort resulted in a compartment full of worried people pointing behind us in the opposite direction from where we were headed, shrugging and shaking heads.

Shit! We missed our stop.

"It's no big deal," I said to Dana, overcompensating in my best Mary Poppins voice, trying to calm his nerves. "We'll just get off on the next stop, then jump on the train headed in the opposite direction."

Dana rolled his eyes.

When the train finally stopped about a half hour later and many miles from where we needed to be, I lunged for the door, holding it open while Dana schlepped bag after bag after bag onto the platform. Once again, we heaved our luggage up and down stairs, to the depot, to find out when the next train would be coming.

Just as we approached the rickety little building, the lights went out, and the train conductor, carrying his old-fashioned lunch pail and thermos, with his jangle of keys, locked the door behind him.

My heart sank.

Not deterred, I said in my hybrid Spanish/Italian, "Sir, we missed our stop. When's the next train?"

He pointed to a bench, on the other side of the tracks, shook his head, and mumbled words I interpreted as "Stupid Americans, go wait over there for the train." Then he climbed into his tiny European toy car that made a Mini Cooper look like an Escalade and burned rubber, leaving us in his dust.

In stunned silence, Dana and I scratched our heads. Then finally, reluctantly, we schlepped our monstrous bags up and down stairs until we arrived on the deserted island between train tracks. With not another soul in sight, we sat and waited, until the few lights in the distance, one by one, began to extinguish. I gasped, peering up and down the tracks, seeing nothing but pitch darkness.

Dana and I looked at each other with wide eyes and the realization: there was no train coming to get us . . . until tomorrow.

We both frantically tried to call an Uber or taxi to rescue us, but we were in a dead zone, and I hoped that wouldn't be literal. In spite of us being on the outskirts of the fashion capital of the world, it felt like we were in a place time forgot.

Dana began to cuss under his breath, "Why did I ever let you talk me into flying out of Milan? I knew we should've flown out of Rome . . ."

Though desperate to stay positive, I couldn't help but think, *OK, this is how we'll die. Someone is going to spot us with our ten thousand expensive-looking bags, and we will be robbed, and I will be raped, and we will be murdered. Or maybe we both will be raped . . . Holy God, please help us!*

That's when it happened. I belted out to the crickets in my best gravely, twangy Janis Joplin impersonation, "Busted flat in Baton Rouge, waiting for a train, feeling near as faded as my jeans . . ."

Dana didn't find it funny, but singing made me laugh.

"Hey, if we're going to die, we might as well go out laughing."

Just then, in the distance, in the dappled darkness, I spotted a hunched figure making its way toward us.

As he approached, about twenty feet away, my heart clenched as I recognized him. He was the *Despicable Me* villain, Gru, from the train.

I leaped from the bench, survival mode kicking in at full tilt, conjuring all the fake buoyancy of a thousand cheerleading squads. "Hola! Hablas Español?" I asked if he spoke Spanish, hoping it would score us points and dissuade him from killing us.

He responded in a surprised, raspy, "Sí, un poquito." (Yes, a little.) Then, in Spanish tinged with an Italian accent, he asked us, "Necesitas que te lleven?"

I whispered to Dana, "He's asking us if we need a ride."

Dana responded a hasty, "No, we're fine."

I flashed Dana a severe look and said under my breath, "No. Dana. We. Are. Not. Fine. Look, we're either going to die here on this abandoned train platform by some unknown person, or we'll die at the hands of someone we now know. He seems like the lesser of two evils. I say we go with him."

Dana grumbled more cuss words under his breath, and the next thing I knew, Gru picked up three of our heaviest bags like they were feathers, and, like lambs to slaughter, Dana and I followed, carrying our lighter bags across the tracks, up and down the stairs, eventually to the nearly deserted parking lot. When we arrived at the only vehicle left, I prayed, *Please don't be creepy.* Then Gru opened the door of the long, black sedan. Sure enough, his serial-killer-mobile was a hearse. It doesn't get creepier than that.

He hoisted our bags into the back near mud-caked shoes where a coffin containing a dead body must've once laid, as I tried not to let my inner ewwww show.

Dana and I trepidatiously walked around to the passenger side of the truck, locking eyes, reading each other's minds. *This is it. . . . We can make a run for it. . . . We'd lose our bags, including all the equipment and footage that's been shot, but possibly save our lives . . . or do we surrender to our fate?* We both shrugged—we'd come this far. We argued in whispers about who should sit next to Gru. It seemed to make sense (to Dana) that I sit in the middle. "It was your idea to go with him," he whispered.

"Thanks for pimping me out," I snarked. "Fine."

I squeezed in between my husband and the scary man. As we drove, I pulled out my phone and thankfully could see one lonely flickering bar of connectivity. I pulled up the driving directions to our hotel. I showed Gru the map that said turn right. I followed by saying, "*Gire a la derecha.*" Gru waved me and my phone away with an annoyed look on his face. My stomach dropped when he turned left. My GPS kept redirecting and redirecting, but I could see Gru becoming increasingly angry at the constant chirping. Not wanting to upset our captor, I turned off the volume. Dana and I shared hopeless looks of defeat, like prisoners being forced to walk to a guillotine.

Then the thought popped in my head from a police show I'd watched years before: *if a killer knows your name, it humanizes you to them, making them less inclined to hurt or kill you.* So, I blurted in my broken Spanish/Italian, "Il mio nome è Kelly y mi esposo es Dana.

Come ti nombre?" ("My name is Kelly, and my husband is Dana. What's your name?")

Gru grunted without looking up from the road ahead. "Il mio nome è Fati." ("My name is Fati.")

"Fati. Mucho gusto piacere encontrarte." ("Nice to meet you.") "Grazie mille por ayudundandonos. Estamos muy agradecidos." ("Thank you for helping us. We're really grateful.") I continued to ramble, to which he replied with more grunts and single-syllabic words.

He seemed fixated on taking us somewhere, to a place I didn't know. We were totally helpless. As Fati maneuvered through the dark streets, I closed my eyes and sent out a silent all-points bulletin to all angels, not just the ones assigned to me, but all of them.

The next thing I knew, Fati pulled in front of a brightly lit hotel, with a bellboy in uniform standing out front greeting us by name, "Dana and Kelly," like he was expecting us. Holy God . . . we were at our hotel.

Dana and I looked at each other with a silent glee, mixed with relief, mixed with shock.

Fati didn't bring us somewhere to die. He didn't kill us. Before climbing out of the car, I threw my arms around Fati, thanking him profusely for rescuing us (and for not murdering us— I added with my inside-Spanish/ Italian).

Instinctively, I reached into my pocket to hand him all the euros I had on hand. This was when he looked at me then like he was truly going to kill me. Angrily knitting his brows together, insulted, he spat, "No!"

"But how else can we thank you?" I asked, "Are you . . . hungry? Would you like to join us for dinner?" His face brightened, and his eyes twinkled like a little boy's on Christmas morning, and he nodded. "Yes, *sì!*"

I didn't realize how clenched and unbreathing my body had been for the thirty-minute ride until I stepped onto the sidewalk in the light of the hotel's marque.

We were safe. We were OK.

Fati unloaded our bags out of the back of his hearse. I told Fati to grab a table in the restaurant while we put our bags away.

Once in our room, Dana and I locked the door, then hugged, shook, laughed, and cried. After freshening up, we entered the restaurant. There in the middle of the lovely patio, surrounded by beautiful flowers and fountains, sat our new friend, Fati, upright, reading the menu, with a glowing smile. Dana and I joined him like we were meeting a long-lost friend.

Over delicious spaghetti and chianti, through my broken Spanish/Italian and Fati's Italian/Spanish, the three of us enjoyed a lively conversation, discussing politics, world events, art, and literature. Fati turned out to be the most thoughtful and gentle soul in *Despicable Me* clothing, except when I shared how much I preferred the beauty of the Spanish, French, and Italian languages over English.

Fati hit the table with his fists, shaking the silverware, "No! English best. It language of freedom. You lucky from USA!" he reprimanded in surprisingly discernable English.

In shock, I saw myself through his eyes: an entitled woman who'd been born and raised in freedom in the belief that she could be and do anything. He shared that he was from a large family (nine kids) in a poor region of Tunisia, where his life had been full of struggle. To him (even though he could only speak a little), English was the language of liberation. I couldn't articulate back then how, to me, OGLE is *my* language of liberation.

Here's how I OGLE'd it:

O: *What is the Offending behavior and/or situation?*

Earlier that night I'd been upset that the train stops weren't more clearly marked and that the automatic doors didn't remain open longer. Being left behind triggered feelings of helplessness and terror. What turned out to be most offensive (despicable), however, was my own negative projection on this wonderful man who turned out to be our hero.

Oh yes, typically when we OGLE, it's because we are offended by another's behavior. But for this one, I had to confront my own offending behavior. Just like Jimmy Buffet's song "Margaritaville"—after blaming everyone else, he eventually comes to realize, "It's my own damn fault."[8] This offending situation would've never happened if it weren't for my own ineptitude that caused us to miss our stop, followed by my negative assumptions that created unnecessary drama.

G: *What is Good about that offending behavior and/or situation?*

Sometimes the best things in life happen as a result of the mistakes we make, the detours we take, and the strange new friends we encounter in the most unexpected places. Our trip to Europe had been incredible, but this last leg of our journey was the best, maybe even the most memorable. I was also humbled to discover the importance of questioning my assumptions—realizing how easily my mind could conjure and believe an inaccurate story based on skin-deep attributes.

L: *How am I peering into the Looking Glass (mirror)?*

Without meaning to, I've left people behind in moments when I've been so single-mindedly focused on the task at hand, getting to the next stop on my journey, trying so hard to stay on track with my goals. The locomotive of my willpower's volition has not always budgeted time to stop, open the doors of my heart, and take inventory of where I am and who I'm with.

There's also a strange hero in me who emerges in extreme situations. The times I've felt the most lost or abandoned, she shows up to reassure me that the universe has my back.

E: *How will I allow this situation to Elevate me? What Elevated action will I take?*

If Fati wanted to, he could've robbed and killed us. But he didn't. Every time I think of him, my appreciation of people, strangers, and life itself amplifies. Years later I read Malcolm Gladwell's *Talking to Strangers*, which affirms we can trust that—despite the few exceptions to the rule—most people are inherently good and trustworthy.

This isn't to say I'm throwing my intuition out the train window. It's the limbic brain's job to profile people, places, and circumstances. However, I'm learning to question my snap judgments while thanking the part of me trying to keep me safe, differentiating fear-based thoughts from true discernment.

Years after arriving home, safe and sound, I learned the concept of *amor fati*—a Latin phrase that does not, as some would assume, mean "love your fat," but, "love your fate." Associated with the late, great German philosopher Friedrich Nietzsche, the Stoics, and

Marcus Aurelius, amor fati describes an attitude in which one sees everything that happens to them, including suffering and loss, as good or, at the very least, necessary.

Besides loving and appreciating our new friend and savior, Fati, amor fati is at the heart of this entire book—the notion that we should not waste our crises but, instead, own them and honor them.

Besides meeting Fati, my favorite takeaway from that trip is that now, when I feel like all is lost, I access my inner Janis Joplin and raise my vibration from hopeless to hopeful. When I'm feeling busted flat, I remember to bust out in my sometimes-off-key (flat) singing voice, and whether I'm in Baton Rouge, Milan, or back home in Los Angeles, I know I'll always find my way back to the right side of the tracks.

Blush-Covered Bruises

Somewhere over Texas

If you don't love yourself, nobody will. Not only that,
but you won't be good at loving anyone else.
Loving starts with the self.

WAYNE DYER

On a quiet airplane halfway between Dallas and Los Angeles, I tried to corral my snotty, sputtering tears. I covered myself with the scratchy complimentary blanket, so the middle-aged woman seated beside me wouldn't catch an eyeful of the makeup-covered purple and red bumps, cuts, scrapes, and bruises confetti-ed across the landscape of my twenty-two-year-old body.

I wasn't marred from an abusive boyfriend but from my own clumsiness. I was the backup dancer for the pop duo Bordeaux, and I was on my way home from a performance at the Texas State Fair.

I deemed it a good show because I "left it all on the stage." It didn't faze me when my unwieldy hair tangled around my hoop earrings. I simply ripped the jewelry out, tearing my earlobe. I accidently pulled out a clump of tangled hair, leaving a trail of blood on the stage, without skipping a beat, literally.

This kind of self-damage was not uncommon for me. I was told dancers were supposed to be graceful—and I could be when I tried, but I treated my body like it was a thing to fling. I took pride in hurling myself into my performances, rolling all over the stage, and knocking into props and scaffolding in my way, in the same way rockstars break their guitars or kick over their amps.

I wrestled in a love-hate relationship with my body, struggling with its powers and its terrors, like a blind person whose only mode of transportation was behind the wheel of a souped-up Ferrari. The perks of being attractive started to show at age eighteen. I was thrilled when the pilot of a 747 invited me to the cockpit to fly the plane. Then, at nineteen, my body got the attention of bouncers who escorted my high-heeled and mini-skirt-clad underage friends and me through throngs of people waiting outside nightclubs in downtown L.A., lifting the red velvet rope—with no cover charge and all the free alcohol we could guzzle.

But I related to my body as if it were a rebellious object hell-bent on being voluptuous instead of willowy like the models in the magazines. I worked hard to be anorexic, but fainting spells gave me away when I deprived myself of food for more than a day. So, I tried in earnest to be bulimic, in hopes of reducing the size of my thick booty and mighty thighs. But this tactic didn't work either because self-induced vomiting burst blood vessels in my eyes, another dead giveaway.

Hating my form, I felt hostile toward it on good days and contempt toward it on bad days. Believing it a misbehaving thing, it didn't occur to me to pamper or protect it. No matter how much I

dieted, exercised, starved, or strangled it
with plastic wrap even on hot summer
days, it refused to be skinny the way
I most wanted it to be. I appreciated
its rhythm and ability to improvise
and entertain when the spotlight was on.
It could turn heads, open doors, elicit catcalls. It even provoked admiration and
sometimes the wrath of women. I was
dammed for not being attractive enough
to be the skinny model I thought I
should be and dammed for being attractive enough to get hate letters in my school
locker the moment I turned eleven and grew
breasts. The worst was nearly getting raped
at age eighteen by a group of guys on a train in
Spain. Were it not for me kicking my way to free-
dom (courtesy of my muscular thighs), I imagine my life would've
turned out very differently. Clumsiness was my passive-aggressive
way of abusing my body because I was upset at it for holding me
hostage in a lose-lose battle.

Under the scratchy blanket, I flipped through the images in *The
Power of Myth* by Joseph Campbell, a birthday gift from a friend.
I was struck by a series of goddess statues and their captions. They
told about how the Greeks honored the female form and literally
placed women's bodies on pedestals. Breasts symbolized nurturing;
the torso symbolized the womb of creation; arms were for holding,
comforting, embracing a world in need; legs were for taking a stand,
protesting injustice; eyes for beholding beauty and visions of what
was to come.[9]

Reading Campbell's words was like unearthing a buried city in
myself. Could the female form—my female form—be something

sacred to revere, to honor, to inspire? I'd never heard of such a notion. Discovering that the female body could be considered holy was like finding out the world wasn't flat but voluptuous and round, like me.

Then this strange sensation overtook me, an iceberg in the center of my chest thawing into hot liquid streaking my face.

What was happening to me?

I continued reading the book until I couldn't see; my eyes had become too blurry with tears as I realized my body wasn't trying to undermine me—she was built the way she was built, and what if that was OK?

I tried to stop my tears, but it was too late. I was filled with hot remorse for the cruelty I'd inflicted upon myself. The concerned lady next to me offered a tissue and a sympathetic look. "Are you OK, honey?"

I accepted her tissue, thanked her, shook my head, then returned to weeping for the remainder of the flight. As the tears continued, I heard my inner voice apologizing to my body for referring to her as an "it," slowly scanning for every bump, cut, and bruise, saying to each one a silent "I'm so sorry."

Here's how I OGLE'd it:

O: *What is the Offending behavior and/or situation?*

The messages I was force-fed by the patriarchal media and the world around me as a young girl growing up in Los Angeles. On top of all the objectification hurled at me on a daily basis, I felt pressured to live up to unrealistic standards of perfection, which led me to treat myself like an object.

G: *What is Good about that offending behavior and/or situation?*

During the time in my life when I had the most self-disregard, I was the most adventurous, risk-taking, daring, and bold. I would've never been accused of being an overly careful Miss Priss.

The spiritual truth is we are more than our bodies. I wasn't coming from a higher perspective back then, but there was something liberating about not overly identifying with my body.

L: *How am I peering into the Looking Glass (mirror)?*

I've been crueler to myself than anyone else has been or could ever be. I've also objectified others—being attracted or repelled by particular physical attributes. It's true, what we're looking at, we're looking with. In other words, we see what we be.

E: *How will I allow this situation to Elevate me? What Elevated action will I take?*

A few months after the plane ride, I was referred to a therapist, who immediately asked me about my bruises. I told her the story I shared above. Then she responded in a voice like honey, "Kelly, you need to make rooooooooom for yourself. Your refusal to honor the space your body needs is a denial of it. This only perpetuates you feeling more and more disassociated and thus attracting people into your life who reflect that back to you. Making rooooom for yourself can begin the process of turning this around."

After I let her wise words sink in, I shared with her a nightmare I had where I was ordered by an angry man to wrap a crying baby in cellophane and shove her in a silverware drawer. My therapist responded, "A nightmare is an unfinished dream. You get to choose your ending."

Empowered, I chose to envision that I rescued the baby, tore the cellophane off, yelled at the man to move out of my way, and comforted the crying baby, telling her I was so sorry and I'd take care of her going forward. My therapist smiled and said my dream reflected that I was rescuing my essence from the abuse I'd allowed and perpetuated.

Then she gave me the assignment to repeat this phrase silently throughout the day, to myself: *I am a hero on a hero's journey.* I felt like sappy *Saturday Night Live* character Stuart Smalley chanting this affirmation, especially because I didn't feel like a hero at all. In fact, I felt like the exact opposite. Yet despite my resistance, over time, this phrase began to sink in—and I started feeling stronger and more integrated. Little by little, with therapy, twelve-step programs, shamans, crystals, meditation, self-help books, and every transformational modality I could get my hands on, I began to heal. In fact, I went to school and became a certified clinical hypnotherapist, with an emphasis on dreamwork.

In the nearly three decades since that airplane ride, even though my life still has its ups and downs, it's a sanctuary of peace, tranquility, and self-love compared to the life I knew back then. In fact, the core of my work was birthed from that breakdown/breakthrough. With support, like a phoenix, I rose from the ashes of my long era of self-abuse, with my dreams and the hero's journey as my trusty companions. A core element of the work I still do today is paying this wisdom forward by supporting people to make rooooooooom for themselves, while reminding them they are heroes on a hero's journey.

Oh yes, I proudly report (gently knocking on wood) I have not a single bruise or blush-covered discoloration on my body.

The Cracked Pot

Southern California

Serenity is not freedom from the storm,
but peace amid the storm.

S. A. JEFFERSON-WRIGHT

After I heard the news my ex-boyfriend Mark was in jail, charged with battery after getting into a barfight, I could not fall back asleep. This was the call I'd prayed would never come.

Even though it had been decades since we'd been a couple, I felt inexplicably responsible for him. I joked that I was his mother in a past life. This may have accounted for our dysfunctional dynamic as romantic partners but our perfect dynamic as friends.

My mind reeled back to when I met him. Me and my just-out-of-high-school gal pals, with fake IDs in hand, found our way into the nether regions of a Hollywood dive bar. He was a motorcycle-riding, jet-black-spikey-haired, tattoo-covered lead singer in a punk/metal band. And I, a former cheerleader, homecoming princess, and good

Catholic girl, fell hard for him as he screamed indecipherable angry lyrics into his microphone at earsplitting decibels.

We were only together a few awkward months before we discovered we were better off platonic. More specifically, he became my first-ever "spiritual counseling" client—long before I'd ever known such a job existed. I was his 9-1-1 call in the middle of the night, for his many rock-bottom moments.

A few years into our friendship, I was awakened in the middle of the night by such a call. He slurred as he told me about how he'd gotten into a brawl with a guy in a bar who'd been mistreating a waitress—"someone had to show him he can't get away with treating women like that." He gave me his usual litany: "I hate people . . . besides you. Give me a reason to stay on the planet."

I scrolled through my metaphysical Rolodex and opened my mouth, and out popped the story of Mitchell May, a survivor of a horrific car crash I'd just heard speak at my church. While in traction, Mitchell was told he'd never walk again since most of the bones in his body weren't just broken but crushed. Before he consented to the amputation of his limbs, a shaman who was offering his counseling support to the hospital's patients entered his hospital room and taught him to shift his attention beyond his physical self to a place far above where he could experience a release from body-identification (aka pain). From there, the shaman instructed Mitchell to look down upon his physical body to see the state of his "egg" (the energy container surrounding his body).

Mitchell reported that it looked like Swiss cheese, full of holes.

The shaman instructed him to envision healing light from God/ Source/the Power of the Universe, filling up and repairing the holes, thus, healing his egg. After several days of intense focus, Mitchell began to "miraculously" show signs of healing. Eventually, not only was he able to keep his limbs and learn to walk again but he resumed living an athletic life.[10]

After a long sigh and some quiet, manly sniffles, Mark croaked, "That was exactly what I needed to hear. Thanks for being my angel."

I never felt drained by our conversations—in fact, I felt what I imagined a heroin rush would feel like for being his hero(ine). And it was addictive, even though the progress he'd make seemed sometimes to be two steps forward, one step back. But after trying my best to help him for so many years and it still leading to jail, I felt like a capital-F Failure. I had no choice but to lay down my broken tools, wave the white flag of defeat, and admit that my best efforts were not enough. Also, harder to face, was the fact that perhaps being his savior had never been my job.

On the phone with Mark a few days after he was bailed out, I was in mid-rant about how he should work harder at controlling his temper.

Mark interrupted, "You don't realize how much I do work my ass off!"

Then he shared with me about the blood and feces smeared on the windows of his cell. That would be horrible for anyone, but it was especially destructive for him. He who has a hound dog's acute senses was surrounded by the odor of vomit, urine, and shit.

He said, "Kelly, I could've spent my time in jail carving more f-words into the walls, but instead I learned the Serenity Prayer."

"What?" I asked.

"The Serenity Prayer was carved into a section of the wall. I stood in front of that prayer for hours, tracing my fingers along the jagged ridges around each letter, reciting it over and over until I memorized it:

God grant me the serenity
To accept the things I cannot change,
Courage to change the things I can,
And wisdom to know the difference.[11]

And then I sat on my disgusting cot, closed my eyes, and did the egg meditation you taught me. I envisioned the egg around each of the screaming dudes in the cells on my floor. . . I pictured their eggs—and they were all cracked. But then I started to see light weaving through their splintered places."

He continued, "Then it was as if I could see light bursting through the walls and ceiling of the jail, and through all the prisoners . . . even the guards, who were just as effed up as the inmates. After a while, I could see light glowing through the cracks of my own egg."

I marinated in his words as I sat perched on the mountaintop ledge overlooking red rocks up the trail near my home. Against an indigo sunset, high above the world, I was blown away by his incredible story. My only response was to reiterate the wisdom of a spiritual teacher I'd once heard: "It's easy to be enlightened, peaceful, and prayerful on a mountaintop. But, if you can find serenity in the midst of hell breaking loose, that's mastery."

How I OGLE'd it:

O: *What is the Offending behavior and/or situation?*

Mark went to jail, and it broke my heart. I feared it would ruin his life. And I felt like all the advice I'd tried to give him over the years was for naught.

G: *What is Good about that offending behavior and/or situation?*

Mark made the most of his time behind bars, memorizing the Serenity Prayer and doing the egg meditation for the healing of all the inmates, including himself.

Mark contributed to my life in a profound way. While I was trying to fix him, he served me back the egg meditation and the Serenity Prayer in a way I'll never forget.

Even though my efforts didn't prevent him from going to jail, I credit him for igniting my passion for the healing arts. Because of him, I was driven to uncover all manner of modalities, technologies, and paradigm-shifting magic pills that I hoped might awaken him to his light and purpose on the planet. But it turns out all the voracious studying I thought had been for him was actually for me.

L: *How am I peering into the Looking Glass (mirror)?*

I also know what blood-curdling rage feels like. I work hard to see that energy as rocket fuel and to redirect it in a positive way, instead of lashing out physically at the person who triggers it. I've learned that reacting tends to make a bad situation irreparably worse.

E: *How will I allow this situation to Elevate me? What Elevated action will I take?*

I regularly practice the egg meditation and the Serenity Prayer, allowing them both to become etched into the concrete of my own prison walls, creating a portal to freedom within myself and to authentic service for others (minus the God complex).

Years later I heard the allegory about a woman with a cracked pot whose job it was to carry water home from the nearby river. She walked back and forth, day after day, but was always dismayed to discover there were only a few drops left when she finally made it home. Even though the folks for whom she intended the water didn't seem to benefit from all her hard work, unbeknownst to her, flowers had grown on the trail from the accidental watering along the way.

So, despite being unsuccessful at rescuing Mark from going to jail, the path I've walked for all these years, without realizing, has become bountiful, with friends and clients whose lives have been enriched. Maybe that was our cracked-pot-soul-agreement all along.

My Breast Friend

Southern California

Lots of people want to ride with you in the limo,
but what you want is someone who will take the bus
with you when the limo breaks down.

OPRAH WINFREY

"My breast has to go in for a biopsy tomorrow. Would you come with me?" asked Jo-e.

Without hesitating or checking my schedule, I blurted, "Of course!"

Jo-e's been the first responder to my 9-1-1 and 4-1-1 calls for the past two decades, always available to lend an ear, a hand, or a smoothie to make life's transitions, well, smoother. So, when she asked for help, I couldn't spout "Yes!" fast enough. Besides, I was terrified they'd find cancer. I was selfishly attached to her being alive, in my corner, for the long haul. And I knew my worry would be lessened if I could be as close to the ring of fire with her as possible.

The next day, I suited up with guns blazing. Oops, wrong image—I actually showed up more like a Disney princess on Ritalin: positive, happy, chipper, with butterflies and little birds landing on my shoulder, everything I thought a friend should be in a situation like this.

Within the sterile scent of rubbing alcohol, under the harsh fluorescent lights, I was grateful the nurse let me into the windowless exam room. As I glanced down upon Jo-e's dainty form clad in a cornflower-blue, crinkly paper robe, she looked up with saucer eyes and asked me to hold her feet for moral support.

"Of course." I scurried over, glad to have a job during such a help-less moment. Beaming reassuringly, holding back tears, I tried to infuse a hopeful drop of humor into the seriousness of the situation. I joked, "I feel so Large Marge right now," causing Jo-e to tee-hee.

Jo-e and I often teased that since I'm a bodacious, Amazonian blonde, my nickname is Large Marge. And since she is a diminutive, brunette mash-up of the best of Marissa Tomei and Frida Kahlo (sans the unibrow), her nickname is Itty Bitty Betty. In this moment, with her on the exam table and me standing over her, our archetypes were exaggerated to cartoonish proportions.

The doctor and nurse entered the room in their stiff, white lab coats and instantly put the kibosh on our irreverent giggling. The doctor pulled up a stool, peered through her glasses at her notes and X-rays. Folding down Jo-e's robe, in red she drew an *X* on my friend's exposed breast to mark the spot where the unwelcome abnormality had been detected.

I squeezed Jo-e's petite feet through her socks, then like out of a horror movie, as if in slow motion, the doctor injected the biggest needle I'd ever seen into the center of the X. As if struck by lightning, Jo-e's pint-size body seized, and she pierced the antiseptic air in pain. The needle hit a nerve, and an electrical current shot through her breast, ricocheting through her feet and into my body. A wave of nausea flooded me, and the room tilted on its side then spun me like it was a carnival ride . . . until all went black.

Distressed voices urged, "LET GO OF HER FEET!"

In my blurry dream, I had no idea who everyone was yelling at, but I wished the dimwit would let go of her damn feet. Crumpled in a heap at the foot of the exam table, peering into white-hot light, I realized I was the dimwit the doctor and nurse were yelling at, who came within inches of pulling their doll-like patient off the exam table and onto the floor with the biopsy needle still in her breast!

I may have lost consciousness, but I never lost my grip, nor my intent to contribute to Jo-e's care in the best way I could . . . and in so doing, I nearly inflicted major damage.

The nurse lifted me off the floor by the arm, like a naughty schoolgirl caught smoking, and shooed me out the door. Apparently, my assistance was no longer needed.

Embarrassed and shocked, I was mostly horrified that I had added more drama to an already dramatic situation. Some help I was. Luckily, my antics didn't cause major damage or interfere with the biopsy.

Jo-e finally emerged into the waiting room, where I was hiding my beet-red face behind a magazine. I bounded over to her, apologizing profusely, "I'm soooo sorry! You asked me here to support you, and instead, I almost hurt you way worse than the ten-foot-long biopsy needle did!"

As I drove home along the beachy city streets of Santa Monica, even though Jo-e was woozy and tender from the whole debacle, that didn't keep her from shushing my blubbering as we OGLE'd what had happened.

O: *What is the Offending behavior and/or situation?*

I blacked out and nearly pulled Jo-e off the exam table.

G: *What is Good about that offending behavior and/or situation?*

Luckily, I unclenched my hands from her feet just in time, before pulling her off the bed, causing her to fall to the floor, impaling her poor boob more than it already was. What was also good about the situation was what Jo-e said: "Kelly, my whole life I've been made to feel like a hypochondriac—everyone thinking I'm exaggerating when I say I'm in pain, or that I'm crying just to get attention. The truth is, I've endured a lot of agony in my life that has gone mostly unrecognized. Feeling alone, even scorned in my pain has added insult to injury—even causing me to question my sanity. But, today, without meaning to, it was like you joined me, and bore witness not just to the excruciating pain from the needle hitting a nerve but, on a parallel plane, to the vein of pain that's run through my life. I'm so sorry you had to feel all that . . . but I'm strangely grateful you did. I feel validated for having such an intense reaction."

"Even though I almost pulled you off the table while you had an arrow sticking out of your boob?" I asked.

"Yes," she said.

"Aw, gee . . . that's why you're my breast friend."

L: *How am I peering into the Looking Glass (mirror)?*

We both talked about how grateful we felt to have thin walls that allow for the ability to step into the skin of another human being. And yet, going around feeling other people's suffering to such a degree that we lose our center is a recipe for disaster. Jo-e recognized, as a holistic health practitioner, that she (in the past) used to take on her clients' issues. This situation, for both of us, underscored the importance of having strong boundaries.

E: *How will I allow this situation to Elevate me? What Elevated action will I take?*

This situation demonstrated the importance of having empathy—the ability to tap into how someone else is feeling—without it engulfing me. In other words, it doesn't do a drowning person any good if the rescuer goes down along with them. The drowning person might feel temporarily comforted, knowing they've got companionship as they sink to a watery grave. But what they really want is someone with a firm tether to the ship to cast a line to pull them back to safety.

My elevated action is to ground myself within the boundaries of my own center. That way I won't give in (so easily) to the undertow of someone else's energy . . . even under the guise of love.

When I shared this with Jo-e, she scoffed, "Boundaries, schmoundaries. I'm grateful you went overboard with me. I feel so lucky you went down with my ship . . . and ultimately there was no damage. It was the most medicinal thing you could've done."

Days later I was grateful to hear the biopsy revealed that Jo-e's cyst was benign.

Over the years, Jo-e has invited me along on several doctor's office and hospital visits . . . virtually . . . from afar . . . or from as close as the waiting room. My prayers and good vibes are still requested, but from a safe physical distance. Which is fine by me.

Years after this incident, on a single day, three separate people shared this Anne Lamott quote with me, which I've since included into my daily meditation repertoire: "Lighthouses don't go running all over an island looking for boats to save; they just stand there shining."[12]

You Can't Plug In Here

Southern California

*When one door of happiness closes, another opens; but often
we look so long at the closed door that we do not see
the one which has been opened for us.*

HELEN KELLER

"Ma'am, you can't plug in here," blurted the barista of the popular chain coffee house (that I shall purposely not name) in West Hollywood.

It was 2004, and this was the coffee house I'd been hunkered in for months, trying to meet my first-ever deadline, on my first-ever book, with my first-ever publisher.

I Had the Strangest Dream. Yes, I did. But that's beside the point. *I Had the Strangest Dream: The Dreamer's Dictionary for the 21st Century* was the name of the book over which I was slaving.

I was overwhelmed by the daunting task of having to churn out a record number of pages under an airtight timeline. Being new to the literary world, I aimed to please my publisher by meeting her outrageous deadline, an amplification of my already-over-the-top people-pleasing personality. I desperately wanted to get an A+ by turning in a polished manuscript on time, so they'd invite me back to write another book, and another. . .

But hard as I tried, I couldn't produce my target page count nestled in my home office. After one or two pages, I'd get sleepy, distracted, or interrupted by my dogs, my husband, the neighbor's blaring leaf-blower, or the need to suddenly get to the gym, give myself a pedicure, make a sandwich, organize my closet, or clean the inside of the chimney.

But the buzz of my local coffee shop and the aromas of buttery-sweet baked croissants and freshly ground coffee beans percolated into my senses and infused me with the focus to churn out twice as many pages as I could at home.

I was perplexed with this completely out-of-character turn of events. I figured I'd misheard the barista, or maybe I'd been spending too much time dreaming all night and writing about dreams all day and was confused. I removed my earbuds. "Ha ha." I peered up from the bluish-amber glow of my computer screen and half-smiled at the millennial with spiky purple hair, multiple piercings, and tattoo sleeves. Why in God's name would he feel the need to invade my space and wreck my flow with his preposterous joke? I turned away from the pesky intruder and tried to pick up where I left off.

He persisted, "Ma'am, I'm not joking. You can't plug your laptop in here."

"Are you serious?" Now I was annoyed. "I . . . I've been writing here for months . . . I order food and coffee." I pointed at my half-eaten blueberry scone and half-drunk latte with my mahogany lipstick smeared around the rim, proof it was mine. "Look at all the other people working on their scripts and books . . . I don't know what you're talking about. Isn't this a coffee house where people come to write?"

"You can write here, but I can't allow you to plug in your laptop," he repeated with a smirk.

My laptop had a battery life of a sputtering geriatric fighting for her last breath. I had to plug her in if I was going to get any work done. I demanded to speak to the manager.

"I am the manager," he retorted, pierced lip in a snarl, tattooed hand on defiant hip.

This had to be a prank. I looked around for hidden cameras. Was Ashton Kutcher punking me? But all I saw were other writers on their laptops not being harassed as they typed, slurped coffee, and nibbled pastries, just as I had been.

Indignant, I tried to keep my inner volcano from spewing hot lava all over him as I packed my laptop in a state of shock. For a reason that made no sense, I was being invited to leave. I was kicked out, shooed away by a rude little twerp who called himself a manager. I refrained from blathering, *I'm normally somebody people want to have around. I've fashioned my entire identity into being someone who never gets asked to leave. In fact, my biggest problem in life is people whining when I can't stay longer. Am I in the twilight zone? WTF!*

Luckily, I had the self-control to keep from tossing my coffee and inner dialogue all over him. Instead, the lesser of the evils, I condensed my venom into a steely glare as I left in a huff. I vaguely recalled the tattooed millennial mumbling, "It's a liability . . . If you lose content from your laptop, you can't hold us responsible . . ."

Whatever! Too little, too late, dude. You just lost a customer! I vowed to never buy coffee there again. They'd be sorry.

As I drove erratically home, a minuscule thought bubble appeared over my head in the form of one of my favorite sayings, "When it's this bizarre you know it's the hand of God."

This led to another thought bubble: *Hmmmm . . . what if this is the Universe's way of telling me I'm not supposed to write there?*

Duh? Ya think? My bruised ego spouted like a bratty teenager.

The thought bubbles continued: *If you trust the Art of Navigation* (a teaching by the late shaman Carlos Castaneda), *you'd know the Universe is always communicating via signs and synchronicities, instructing where to go and where not to go. What if you could trust it?*

Fine, my ego pouted as I screeched in front of my house, *but now what am I going to do? I still have my deadline, and I've totally missed my mark for today.*

On my way into the house, by rote, I opened my mailbox, and interspersed between bills and junk mail were not one, not two, not three or four but *five* brightly colored postcards advertising the grand opening of a brand-new coffee shop in my neighborhood. If there had been only one postcard, I would've tossed it out along with the rest of the junk mail. But I felt compelled to notice five invitations.

According to the postcard, this new coffee house was gorgeous. Not a typical chain but one with an inviting, art deco style. In bold yellow print, the announcement read, "Present this card, and your first coffee and pastry are on us!"

Suddenly infused with the spirit of adventure, even if just to quell my curiosity over the bizarreness of my morning thus far, I turned around. Instead of retreating into the house, I drove a few blocks to check out this new spot.

I approached, marveling at the gorgeous décor, more glorious than the photos, as two handsome men greeted me at the front door as if they'd been expecting me. Sal, dark haired, Latino, and Randy, a blond Norse god—this fabulous couple instantly made me feel like royalty. Like Belle in *Beauty and the Beast*, when all the inanimate objects (candelabra, teacups, armoire) in the castle come to life, I could hear a rousing "Be Our Guest."

Gallantly, they led me on a tour and made me the most delicious caramel almond latte I'd ever had, along with an assortment of scones to sample. They asked me what I was working on, and once I told them, they became so excited, they escorted me to the best table in the house. Randy said, "Our feng shui lady identified this as the vortex in the entire place."

Sal followed, "Here's an outlet if you need to plug in your laptop."

My breath caught in my chest, my eyes misted, and I couldn't hold back my gratitude as I hugged them, my book fairy godfathers. I thanked them for their incredible hospitality, medicine for my bruised ego.

"Let us know whatever you need, and it's our pleasure to get it for you," Sal said.

"Now we'll leave you alone to write your book. Make us proud," said Randy.

I spent the next couple of months in their haven. Ensconced in my new office away from home, in the vortex, at the table they reserved for me, every day I wrote the rest of my book. Thanks to Randy and Sal and their gorgeous coffee house (and the best lattes I ever had) I did get my book in, a day before the deadline. Months later when my book launched, they hosted a book release party for me.

How I OGLE'd it:

O: *What is the Offending behavior and/or situation?*

The manager of the first (chain) coffee house was so rude and made me feel unwelcome and unwanted. He basically threw me out.

G: *What is Good about that offending behavior and/or situation?*

What if I wasn't kicked out of the first coffee house but invited to step away from an ordinary situation and toward an entirely more magnificent place than I could've imagined? I never would've budged had I not been forced to leave. There might have been other postcards in the mail, but I'd been too dense to notice.

Perhaps the Universe had to possess the millennial manager to make me leave.

L: *How am I peering into the Looking Glass (mirror)?*

Even though I've struggled (in the past) with setting boundaries, sometimes it's absolutely necessary to tell people they can't plug in to my circuitry—if I don't have the bandwidth. As much as I try to be generous, I know it's OK to be accused of being ungenerous, sometimes.

E: *How will I allow this situation to Elevate me? What Elevated action will I take?*

I think about my knights in shining barista armor when life doesn't go my way. In fact, every time I get what might be considered a rejection, I think of the manager of the first coffee house telling me not to plug in, and I realize, "Rejection is God's protection." Even when it comes to that which we interpret as rejection from a person we're in love with, a job we thought had our name on it, or a pandemic that flings our lives in a completely different direction than where we thought we were headed, we must remember that the Universe is always hurling us toward the person, place, or situation that will flip our switch in a far superior way than we could've imagined in our wildest dreams.

Aw, Bite Me!

New Mexico

Beware of biting jests; the more truth they carry with them,
the greater wounds they give, the greater smarts they cause,
and the greater scars they leave behind them.

JOHANN KASPAR LAVATER

"You're officially the worst houseguest ever," joked Gini, handing me a margarita.

We clinked our glasses then made our way to reclining rockers on her veranda, admiring the glowing terra cotta sunset. "For the record," I said, taking a sip of the frosty cocktail, "being attacked by a bullmastiff isn't my idea of a good time, either."

But I'm getting ahead of myself . . . let me take you back to a few days earlier . . .

Dana and I were visiting our friend Gini, the proprietor of Garden of the Goddess retreat center in Santa Fe, New Mexico. Years before, we lived on her high-desert land in a yurt on a bed of quartz crystal, surrounded by massive red rock formations, bright-blue skies, fragrant piñon trees, and millions of visible, glowing stars.

The day after we arrived, a debilitating migraine crept upon me like a sniper in the night and put my head into a vise. Pain and nausea rendered me incapable of moving from the couch in Gini's gorgeous guest casita, much less able to socialize. But on the third morning of our stay, I awoke with the sun. To celebrate no longer feeling lopsided, I laced up my sneakers and took myself on a light, nostalgic jog.

As the tangerine sun slowly awakened the desert from its starry slumber, my heart swelled with the symphony of life in this rural neighborhood. Set against the steady beat of my blissful feet crunching gravely pebbles along the red-dust-carpeted trail, morning birds chirped, wind whipped through the cacti, and insects scurried. I marveled at the familiar jutting rocks behind the random assortment of elegant adobe homes and the sweet smell of the sage peppering the landscape.

As I was reaching the crescendo of this Julie Andrews moment, singing to myself, "The desert's alive, with the sound of music. . ." two giant, snarling dogs jumped up against a chain-link fence in the front yard of the pueblo-style home I was jogging by.

My heart clenched. But I reassured myself, "Thank God for the fen—" Just as that thought was rounding the corner on becoming a complete sentence, my eyes noticed in horror one of the dogs desperately squeezing its mountain of a body through the gap between the soft red dirt and the bottom of the fence. The gate was tragically levitating high enough from the ground for this Houdini to escape. Statue still, I watched as the two dogs, one following the other, burst forth from their yard onto the dirt road toward me. Before my frozen mouth could scream for help, the hounds from hell flanked me. Guttural barking ensued along with spit spraying, as they menacingly rose on their hind legs. Then one of them, whom I'll call Cujo, locked its snarling teeth around my right forearm and began thrashing it back and forth.

Time stopped as I was whisked above the helter-skelter scene. A voice, soft as a fleece-covered cloud, comforted, "You're going to be all right. These dogs are being protective of their property, and they see you as a threat. They are just giving you a warning. If they wanted to kill you, they would've gone for your throat, and you'd already be dead."

Suddenly, I was back in my body; the pep talk didn't prevent me from screaming, "HELP!!!" in the loudest screech my voice has ever uttered, surely awakening every soul on that once-peaceful Santa Fe morning. My yelling didn't stop the attack dogs, but it thankfully awakened their caretaker. The next thing I knew, a muscled man with a crew cut opened his gate and toppled over himself as he ran, thankfully calling off the dogs. Cujo reluctantly unhinged his knife-like teeth from my bleeding, mauled arm, and both dogs did the walk of shame past their master, back through the open gate with their tails literally between their legs.

The man yelled out to me, "Are you OK?"

Just as I was about to respond with an automatic, "Yes," in the movie screen in my head, I saw the face of a Franciscan monk I'd met who had worked closely with Mother Theresa and had a gift for helping people move through the most heinous of atrocities (war, abuse, severe poverty). His simple method was to encourage people to model after animals in the way they naturally "shake off" trauma. He gave the example of ducks in a pond fighting over a fish. The moment the fight ends, the ducks swim away from each other and let the stress tremor through their bodies and out through their ruffled feathers. They physically shake. Then, moments later, they cruise along, smooth sailing on the pond, as if nothing had ever happened.

The monk said, "The simple act of shaking for a minute or two once we're safe from the unfortunate incident helps us to release the stress hormones and keeps them from lodging into our nerves, leaving us with anxiety. If we could allow our bodies to do this, the trauma would be over, and we would not need to drag it behind us, like an albatross, for the rest of our lives."

In an instant, I realized I was at a crossroads—I was safely out of harm's way, and yet, I was attempting to do what I had always done: suck it up, hold in my pain so as to not heap my troubles on anybody or look like a wimp. I argued with the monk in my mind, *I don't want to lose it in front of this guy. I'll look like an imbecile.*

The monk in my mind chimed in, *Really? Under the guise of trying to look cool to this stranger—whose dog just attacked you—you're going to allow yourself to spend the next twenty-five years in therapy and have panic attacks every time you see a large dog?*

I realized he had a point . . . so, in a flash, I gave it a try. I had nothing to lose, so I unleashed the beast. I uncorked and let my body flail, the tears flowed as the muscled man watched my emotional tsunami in horror (no doubt needing his own trauma-release session to process witnessing my emotional meltdown).

After the minute or two of sobbing and thrashing, I felt surprisingly light. I could feel the gentle hum of the earth, my heartbeat calmed, and the birds resumed their morning song. Aside from needing to elevate my throbbing arm, there was a surprising spring in my step as I floated back to my former residence. Dana freaked out when he saw me, but I reassured him I was OK—truly, not the fake kind. Dana rallied our dear friends to meet us at urgent care. They did an expert job distracting me with humor as I got my arm cleaned and bandaged, followed by rabies and tetanus vaccines. We all dined afterward at our favorite Thai restaurant. As I enjoyed our conversation over delicious tom kha gai (coconut and ginger) soup, I realized I hadn't given my arm a thought for nearly an hour.

Back at Gini's place that night, on her porch, margarita in hand, after she jokingly accused me of being a drama queen and the worst house guest ever for spending my first two days nauseous on her couch then getting attacked by a dog, I quipped, "I believe it was you who named this place Garden of the Goddess. With a name and intent like that, you and your guests shouldn't expect it to be a Club Med vacay—you are the one who set this place up to be a vortex of transformation, not me." With that, we laughed and drank, and I marveled at what a good time I was able to have after such a nightmarish morning.

A few weeks later, back home in Los Angeles, I was on a jog on the trail by my house. Just as I was comparing the scab on my arm to a fall leaf preparing to cascade off its branch, a woman with not one but two bullmastiffs approached. It wasn't until we passed each other with a friendly nod that I took inventory of the absence of heart palpitations, no discernable contraction in my chest, and the fact I wasn't holding my breath.

The monk's technique worked. Shaking out the trauma in real time (as soon as the threat was gone) was the answer. I was shocked at how my ego's need to (try to) look cool could've come at such a cost—potentially rendering me with untold consequences of PTSD.

How I OGLE'd this . . .

O: *What is the Offending behavior and/or situation?*

Being physically attacked. The dog owner didn't have a proper fence to keep his menacing dogs at bay.

G: *What' is Good about that offending behavior and/or situation?*

Had I been a true threat, those dogs would've saved their house from robbery. Protectiveness is important when it's called for, and unfortunately, in this world, sometimes it is called for.

What's good about having an insufficient fence? An insufficient fence is better than no fence at all. Sometimes we don't know our fence is inadequate until something like this happens. Maybe, because of what happened, a new fence will prevent a more tragic circumstance from happening in the future.

L: *How am I peering into the Looking Glass (mirror)?*

Over the years, I've been my worst critic. I've attacked myself worse than those dogs ever could've. Also, with the people I love the most, like my husband, I've allowed my inner dogs to snarl, bite, and thrash when my inner fence wasn't well equipped enough to guard him from my overreactive protective mechanisms.

E: *How will I allow this situation to Elevate me? What Elevated action will I take?*

I had a chance to put into practice what the monk taught me and learned from an indelible experience the validity of releasing emotions in real time. Since my intention in life is to become lighter as I live, not more heavily burdened with baggage and scar tissue as I go, this lesson has been so precious to me. Additionally, since this happened, I've been less of an attack dog to my husband and to myself.

I have stronger fences/boundaries so I can respond in more mature, less hysterical and destructive ways.

It's now years later, and I cherish the scar over the slight indentation on my arm. Like a tattoo, it is a sacred souvenir from that day, and I revere it because every time I touch it, it reminds me it's possible for me, and for all of us, to go through a perilous circumstance and return to peace without undue trauma relatively quickly.

All we have to do is invite the ego to step aside and close our eyes for a minute while we do a crazy dance, shake a tail feather, and convulse the trauma out of our bodies. Who knows, maybe this practice will catch on, and it will one day be cool not to be cool. Until then, if anyone looks at us like we're weirdos, we can just tell them as sweetly as possible, "Aw, bite me!"

There's No Place Like Ommmmm[13]

Southern California

It is the acid test of nonviolence that in a nonviolent conflict
there is no rancor left behind, and in the end
the enemies are converted into friends.

GANDHI

The day before the Los Angeles Women's March in 2016, I received a frantic email from a friend warning me to "be prepared—it might get ugly."

She urged me to take heed of her list of strategies to avoid getting swept up in the potential violence. Her list included the following:

- Write your name and an emergency contact phone number in black marker on your arm in case you get caught in a police raid. If the scene gets televised, someone might be able to see your name and number and bail you out.

- Stay out of the center of the frenzy.

- Be careful!

She shared how her sister had recently been holding hands in prayer with a group of activists in a peaceful protest and had been shot in the eye with a rubber bullet. We talked about those who'd showed up to march over the years around the world and had been run over by tanks, thrown in prison, some even shot and killed. My husband's uncle Don (a Christian minister in Chicago) had marched and gone to jail with Martin Luther King Jr., receiving multiple death threats at his home because of his public stance on civil rights.

With this dark lightning cloud hovering, my friends and I gathered on the eve of the Women's March in a ceremony that included prayer, meditation, and soul-to-soul sharing, plus gobs of chocolate (because, chocolate—well, no need to explain).

We all expressed how devastated and beaten down we felt about the election . . . and how scared, nervous, and unsure we felt about the march the next morning. We questioned if potentially putting our lives at risk was worth it. We all decided it was important to show up anyway. And nothing was going to stop us from marching.

Until then, I'd not been the type to be politically active, except for attending several Marianne Williamson for President rallies, and I'd always taken a very strong stance in the Pepsi/Coke debate. (Go, Coke!)

I'd also suffered from a severe lifelong case of the "disease to please," which was why I'd not been more vocal about my political leanings. I cared way too much about not offending anyone and wanting everyone to think I was the nicest person on the planet. Thankfully, that is no longer the case.

I'd be lying if I said it didn't hurt my feelings when people unfriended or unfollowed me on social media (especially when it was my own family), but I've come to peace with it. In my woman's circle, we've come to trust that the power of sharing our burdens (even without a sense of what the solution might be) always provides at least some measure of a healing alchemy.

By the time we arrived by train in downtown Santa Monica the next morning, we were buoyant, our tanks were full, and we were ready to take on the day come what may, even if that meant—God forbid—getting shot in the eye with a rubber bullet.

We were among thousands of mostly women and some men and children, all packed like intimate sardines into the train compartments. We were smooshed against the bodies of strangers with barely a whisper of personal space on all sides. The metro was programmed to stop at all twenty-five stations along the route to downtown. Every time we'd screech to a pause, the doors would slide open, revealing a sea of eager people, each hoping to find a sliver of space for themselves, to no avail. Crestfallen upon seeing how crammed in we were, despite their disappointment at having to wait for the next train, almost in unison, they encouraged us as we pulled off toward the next station.

Luckily, we were a jovial bunch. I joked, "We're definitely getting our daily hug quota today. At least we're all good sports about this."

I spoke too soon.

At the next stop, a huge, irate man barged his way into our compartment. Like a punk rocker in a slam pit, he started yelling, "MAKE ROOM, YOU SELFISH IDIOTS. THERE'S ENOUGH ROOM. DON'T BE SO SELFISH!"

In an instant, our happy Girl Scout camp became fraught with screaming, yelling, and pushing. The louder people shouted at the man, the more adrenalized he became. I realized there was no fighting this by adding more kindling. This ugly scene would only continue to escalate, so I did the only thing in my power I could think of to do in that moment . . .

I ommmmmed . . . loudly.

Because my friends and I were so on the same wavelength from our ceremony the previous night, they instantly jumped on my om bandwagon. Our voices joined into one mighty organism, and together our ommmmm escalated . . . inciting the rest of our compartment to join. In a blink, we'd become a single voice of the loudest ommmmm I'd ever heard.

I've ommmmmed a lot in my day, but I've never ommmmmed like that . . . with such intensity . . . at such a volume . . . with such a purpose: to snuff out fear with love. This was no light-and-fluffy om. It was an om on a mission.

After about eight rounds of ommmmming, as if we all shared one mind, we gently lowered our volume; the man had stopped ranting for the moment.

Silence settled in upon our compartment. We felt a cautious optimism about having successfully snuffed out the rage, but we didn't know for sure. Once we stepped off the train in downtown, we all took a deep sigh of relief because our collective om had put out the fire.

Gratefully, the incident with the man was the only troubling event during the entire Women's March. In fact, the march itself was incredibly peaceful and good spirited. My sister

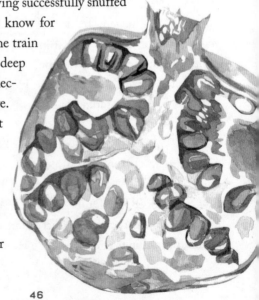

summed it up by saying, "It was like being on the winning team at a sporting event." We felt like we won because we all had an opportunity to have our voices heard and to be shoulder to shoulder with thousands of people gathered (and millions worldwide) who realized how powerful we can be when we join our voices (literally and symbolically) to ensure that peace, freedom, and liberty have a voice (or at least a loud ommmmm).

Here's how I OGLE'd it:

O: *What is the Offending behavior and/or situation?*

The out-of-control rageful energy of the man on the train was terrifying. The rest of us were all feeling vulnerable and scared, and his behavior was like a lit match on a windy day in a dry forest at the height of summer.

G: *What is Good about that offending behavior and/or situation?*

He must've looked inside the train compartment, and seeing there was no room for him, it must have hit his trauma button. Even though his reaction was violent and misplaced, the internal struggle to fight for one's right to have a place in the world is a worthy one.

L: *How am I peering into the Looking Glass (mirror)?*

I can relate to the horrible feeling of being left out. As a shy kid in school, I felt left out (excluded was the word I learned way back then). And there's been many times doors closed on me I thought should've opened, and I took it personally. Even if my response was internal, whereas this man's reaction was external, I can still relate to what I imagine triggered him.

E: *How will I allow this situation to Elevate me? What Elevated action will I take?*

A few days after the event, I was sharing what happened with a friend who worked at my local bookstore. In turn, she told me a story about the Singing Revolution[14] that took place in her native Estonia back in 1988. Even though she was a little girl then, she remembered holding hands with her mother and grandmother, standing in solidarity with one hundred thousand other people from Latvia and Lithuania, singing their song of independence over and over for five days. "It was the most incredible thing," she said wistfully, with tears pooling in her crystalline eyes, "to witness the power of our collective voices to break us free from the bonds of the tyranny."

We then discussed how Martin Luther King Jr and Gandhi taught that nonviolence is not merely the absence of violence but a force unto itself, a soul force, stronger than hate and fear—a force that, if engaged with, will have the final word.

For the first time in my life, I felt the power of nonviolence, not just the intellectual understanding of it. As I think about the irate man, my heart wells with compassion because I imagine he must be troubled to carry around that level of incendiary rage. For my girlfriends and me, he was a strange angel who taught us how powerful we can be in the face of hate. Dorothy said it best when she realized the great, terrifying, and powerful Oz was just a little man with a big God complex. In the end, all she needed to do to get back to her place of power was to tap her heels three times and say, "There's no place like . . . ommmmm!"

The Burning Bougainvillea[15]

Southern California

*The world is a mirror, forever reflecting
what you are doing within yourself.*

NEVILLE GODDARD

It was the summer of 1996, and the low *boom, boom, boom* from the bright-blue lowrider's speakers rattled the pavement I was jogging on, shaking my internal electrical circuitry. Someone whistled, made a harsh slurping sound, and a voice yelled, "Hey, baby. You look fine in those shorts."

The catcalls grew louder as the car approached, driving alongside me as I sprinted. Moving as fast as I could, heart racing as they matched my pace, I looked forward. I heard my schoolteacher mother's voice in my head urge, "If you ignore them, they'll leave you alone."

The driver, who had a black bandana around his forehead, yelled out the window, "Don't be stuck up, Blondie; we're talking to you!" I glimpsed their lustful faces out of my peripheral vision—trouble.

At the opening of the park, I cut a sharp left, trying to escape them. My hands became fists, and the bionic speed of adrenaline infused my veins. Running—harder—under the shaded canopy, speckles of dark-and-light green glinting off the crowns of trees where, thankfully, cars could not follow.

Then I heard a horrible scrape.

Turning my head, I got a quick glance of the guys trying to drive their loud, blue car into the park—but luckily, the undercarriage of their lowrider would not allow them to summit the curb. The crunch of metal on concrete stopped them cold.

But my relief was short-lived. I heard their engine rev, and through the trees, I could see them speed off. I prayed they weren't trying to head me off at the opposite end of the public garden.

I was pure, wide-eyed adrenaline, sprinting with power beyond my ability along the bushes lining the inside, my running shoes, smudged white, flashing over the worn, dirt path, uneven with protruding roots. Glancing down to make sure I didn't trip, my strategy was to keep as close to the trees as possible, staying on the innermost trail. This way, the men wouldn't be able to see me from either side.

Then it occurred to me they might have ditched their car and entered the park on foot, toward me. Right here.

Suddenly, I wasn't safe, again. I wondered if I ever would be. Memories of other threats and assaults deluged my terrified soul.

I felt hot fury at God. I didn't know what there was left to do. I'd been living on the straight and narrow and in therapy—doing every restorative mind/body/spirit practice modality L.A. had to offer, paying my bills, working an honest job as the hostess of a restaurant five days and forty hours a week. And yet it seemed that instead of my life turning out better, like it was supposed to, all this work seemed to be having the reverse effect. It seemed every man I encountered turned sooner or later into a bloodthirsty predator treating me like a juicy steak right off the grill.

No longer trying to be discreet or quiet, not thinking or giving up, I cried out internally, like an animal in rage, at God for making this world such an unsafe place for women. "God, if you're here, which I sincerely doubt," I said to the dirt at my feet, which were now only walking, stepping slowly, "if you want to keep me here on the planet, you better do something, because I can't take this anymore!"

Just then, I was stopped cold in my tracks. I could no longer hear the bass of the lowrider car or any crackling of leaves alerting me of anyone approaching. I took in a deep breath of relief. Then something inside told me to turn around. And when I did, I became thunderstruck . . . not by the men I'd been running from but by the brightest fuchsia-magenta leaves I'd ever seen. I beheld a glorious bougainvillea bush, leaves fluttering in the wind, hyper-bright, as if lit from within.

The technicolor plant must have been twenty feet tall, and its sheer gloriousness completely overtook my senses. City girl that I was, I'd never felt such a profound connection to nature before. But this bougainvillea was no ordinary plant—it exuded a beauty I'd never seen or felt before in nature. It felt like it was reaching out to me, to hug me, heal me, comfort me.

The breeze was sweet. My tears and worry about the men in the lowrider were overtaken by warm awe, as if by magic. I took in a gulp of the delicious, mossy air, and my arms involuntarily rose from my sides, as if tied to helium balloons. I felt the buoyant energy of a dance—and I wondered how it was possible I'd jogged through this park over a hundred times in the year I'd lived there and I had never consciously encountered this violet-pink spectacle. Every moment I stood in the presence of this unexpected delight mended my tired heart, and my fear washed away along with the awareness that my life was no longer in danger. I somehow knew I was OK.

As the sun began its radiant descent, I could feel it was time to go. Yet I wanted so badly for this feeling of healing to last. Without thinking about it, I reached out and broke off a sprig of the bright-pinkish-, red-, purple-glowing bloom. I wanted to carry it with me as a reminder of the bliss I was feeling, in hopes the leaves' healing would stay with me.

Here's how I OGLE'd it:

O: *What is the Offending behavior and/or situation?*

Those men objectified me, terrifying me, treating me like I was prey.

G: *What is Good about that offending behavior and/or situation?*

Jogging home, gratitude washed over me like a wave of kindness. I was thankful that I'd been able to sidestep disaster, once again, and that I somehow kept my wits about me during an incredibly scary moment. The silver lining of this negative experience was that I wound up in a part of the park I'd never seen before, so I could meet the simple miracle of creation. Tears of fresh gratitude fell off my cheeks like raindrops to the pavement.

L: *How am I peering into the Looking Glass (mirror)?*

Then, like turning a dimmer switch from dark to one hundred watts, I was struck with the realization: I'm just like them.

Looking at the bougainvillea was a gift for my senses, but that wasn't enough. Because I was so parched, without asking permission,

I took a piece of it with me, killing a little bit of it in hopes of making the moment last.

I imagined the lowriders and I had been doing the same thing. Masking the excruciating pain of brokenness and the hunger that comes from missing a genuine connection to the Divine propelled us to seek to fill the chasm—we took something we deemed beautiful to fill our emptiness.

To the lowriders, I was nothing more than a brightly colored bougainvillea, something they considered lovely—I was beauty to own, to claim, to take with them.

I wanted the bouganvillea petals because they made me feel alive, connected to the elixir I craved—and I felt entitled to that feeling. So, I took it . . . without asking. It wasn't personal. When I snapped the branch, I wasn't trying to hurt it, make it feel bad, or leave it traumatized. In fact, my taking a part of it was a compliment, as if to say, "I want this

P.S. I realize this is an incredibly sensitive subject; equating these men chasing me to me snapping a sprig off a bush is not the same thing. I am not condoning their behavior, nor am I making light of it, nor making myself culpable. I'm simply sharing the fact that I was able to see a speck of their behavior in me, in the same way that a drop of a virus can inoculate us from getting sick because it contains a microdose of that virus. All I know is this experience marked the beginning of a chain reaction of profound transformation within me . . . and I hope it will for you too.

beauty for my own. I've lost access to mine—but this might help me find it."

Strangely, feeling connected to the men made me feel better. It was a connection I had never made before—me and predatory men, predatory men and me. But in the glow of this moment, I felt freer as I ran. Seeing the common denominator that united us made me feel stronger than before, when I had thought of them as separate from me. Understanding the men's desire helped me fear it a little less.

I was just like them. They symbolized the part of myself who'd forgotten my own beauty, my inexorable connection with Life. I didn't need to be afraid of them as I would be with unfamiliar beasts.

E: *How will I allow this situation to Elevate me? What Elevated action will I take?*

I saw if I couldn't contain bright beauty myself, I would have to seek it externally and ultimately come out feeling empty. The external pursuit comes with a consequence. Maybe this is why the world is in the shape it is. If we go around stripping every tree of its flowers . . . if men go around raping and abducting every attractive girl they see . . . taking resources we deem we need from whomever has it . . . we end up in a world like the one we're living in now.

We grab and take until we realize life is our mirror.

We see what we be.

I wouldn't recognize the gloriousness of that fiery bush unless it was, on some level, within me. I hadn't owned it, yet. But if I did, I'd know, because I would no longer feel the need to take a piece of it.

I craved the wherewithal to stand in beauty's breathtaking presence, to inhale it, to be energized by it—and to move on, holding no material treasure but with an extra spring in my step because I had been reminded of the majesty within me.

Just like that, the spell was broken.

Like a curse that had been a familiar part of my world for years, like a couch in my apartment, a fixture, the feeling of victimhood regarding men's lust had become an ordinary aspect of reality I'd taken for granted. Like it or not, it would always be there, I'd believed. But, encountering the sharp edge of my new clarity, my old victimhood turned out to be a flimsy bubble. Once it popped, it was simply gone.

A couple of years later, driving home from a party around midnight, I wasn't paying attention. Accidently taking a series of wrong turns, I found myself in the bowels of downtown L.A.—in exactly the neighborhood I knew to do everything in my power to avoid. Squinting at a bent sign, I saw a prostitute in a short, red, latex skirt bend over and lean into the open window of an idling car.

White-knuckling the steering wheel, I tried to seize control of the situation. I prayed not to be noticed as I passed a concrete wall of spray-painted graffiti, with bullet holes through smudged windows encased by protective bars. But as I coasted too slowly, trying to get my bearings, a homeless man with a long, gray, dreadlocked beard who was squatting next to a filthy tarp-covered shopping cart flipped me off—as my headlights shined on him while he defecated.

I need to get out of here!

Then—as if on cue, the world's dark answer: something awful happened. I froze in horror as thick smoke began to billow from beneath my hood and the indicator light on my panel blinked on, a bright-red curse. My car was overheating, here in the hairiest part of the armpit of gang territory, of all places. I whispered, "God, please help me," but in the dark sea of barbwire-wrapped buildings, no miracle of safe haven appeared. Had this taken place a year later, I would've had my first cell phone and could've called AAA for help. But, alas, I was alone in an unfortunate circumstance.

Hyperalert and terrified, I rolled my car into a dark corner of a lonely, skeletal gas station. At the back, I found a pit-stop island advertising water and air for tires.

I fumbled with my keys, putting them in my pocket—hoping I wouldn't need to use them as a weapon. As I unlocked the driver's side door, I cursed myself for neglecting to bring the pepper spray keychain my mother had given me. My senses were screaming at me to stay in the car—but I knew I had to lift my hood so the engine could cool off, my only way out of here.

My heart thundered as I stood. I smoothed my skirt, wobbled on the uneven asphalt like a fawn learning to walk. My high-heeled boots stepped in something gooey that smelled rotten. In my shadow, I saw the silhouette of myself, and I quickly wrangled my bushy, blond hair into a low ponytail to be slightly less of a yellow-lit sign announcing FEMALE. My nostrils filled with the rank scent of burnt metal as I opened the hood, letting smoke escape from my enflamed engine.

Before I could scurry back toward the relative safety of the vehicle's interior, the sound of asphalt and gravel crunching beneath feet made me glance up. Two muscular men were strutting right toward the dark corner of the abandoned service station where I stood, literally cornered, caught, with nowhere to run.

As they approached, beating them to the punch, I surprised myself when I called out, "Thank God you're here! Thank you for seeing me and my car all the way back here." My chipper attitude seemed to shock them, and myself. "I'm so clueless when it comes to cars," I went on. "Do either of you guys know the best way to fix an over-heating engine?"

Despite the panic I felt, what happened next blindsided me; in a flash, their faces turned from menacing, to surprised, to friendly. I stuck out my hand, introduced myself, and asked their names.

"Gabriel and Uriel," the bigger one answered, his tone warm.

"Wow, archangels!" I exclaimed. "It must be my lucky night."

My two new guardian angels got to work under my hood, fixing my car so it would be drivable. As they worked, they told me they were mechanics and gave me big-brotherly advice on what to say to the guys at the shop I'd take my car to the next day. Uriel, the trimmer man, gave me the directions I needed to get safely back on the freeway. "This area is dangerous," he cautioned me, my champion. "You shouldn't come here at night. Be careful, eh?" The protective sound of his voice moved me.

"I promise." Then I hugged Gabriel and Uriel warmly, telling them, "I grew up with all sisters, always wishing I had brothers to protect me. Thank you for being my brothers tonight."

As I drove off, waving and smiling, I felt powerful. Reaching the freeway, I shuddered—thinking how this situation might have gone before my bougainvillea experience.

I thought how my "burning bush" from years before not only helped me recognize the importance of safety and consent but helped me to see that there are other ways of approaching dangerous situations that may change their outcome. If I can stop perceiving the enemy in perfectly good men, I might also remember that I can bring out the chivalry in men who might have had trouble on their minds.

As I drove down the freeway, I called to mind the controversial words of A. Justin Sterling, the facilitator of a relationship workshop I'd recently attended. Much to the ruffled feathers of me and the other women in audience, he said, "Most women have no idea the power they hold over men. Not in every case, but in most, women evoke their *valiance* or *violence*."[16]

I hadn't understood what he meant until that moment, but I suddenly became aware that I'd not had a predatory incident with men since my bougainvillea encounter. That experience had so radically changed the lens through which I saw men, it was as if the entire male species got the memo to transform toxic masculinity to sacred masculinity.

No longer seeing men as villains and myself as victim, I felt suddenly strong, taking back the power I hadn't realized I'd given away. Altering the way I see men—no longer as other but now as brother—has led to me feeling safe, which has led to me becoming safe.

Tendral[17]

Southern California & Florida

There is but one freedom, to put oneself right with death.
After that everything is possible.

ALBERT CAMUS

"Tendral is dead."

That was the bomb dropped by the voice on the other end of the phone. Just a few simple words uttered and my bright world, like an overflowing vase with too many roses, tipped and shattered on harsh concrete.

Weeks before, Dana and I had been the happiest we'd ever been in our then six years of marriage. Walking hand in hand barefoot on the sparkling-white, sticky-sand beach at sunset, salty water sloshing on our feet, in front of our philanthropist friend/business partner's gorgeous Florida home. My good friend invited us to stay in her posh digs while we secured funding for our nonprofit organization the Dream Project—a youth empowerment program connecting inner-city kids with the United Nations. I felt like the luckiest girl in the world.

Simultaneous to our arrival, my friend invited a holy man to join us, along with two nannies from his orphanage in India and the baby he'd just rescued. Six-month-old Tendral had been left to die because she'd been born with a double cleft palate, which was bad karma, according to the beliefs of her poor Himalayan village. While visiting the village, the man heard the baby's searing cries. Curious, he followed the sound like a detective. In a dark shed on the outskirts, he discovered the infant disowned, forgotten, lest the community be cursed.

He fell to his knees in recognition that she was a Bodhisattva— one who chooses a difficult life so they may emerge with a wealth of compassion and enlightenment that can bless the world, like a lotus that grows from the deepest mud. He scooped her up, cooing and comforting her. "I'll take care of you, little one."

Although she'd been abandoned, he requested permission of the baby's parents. They were grateful there might be hope for the "cursed baby." He swaddled her, placed her gently in his straw backpack, and carried her to his orphanage.

Due to the cracks in her lips, she was barely able to receive nourishment and was hanging on to life, like a quivering tendril of vine. Once safely at his orphanage in India, the holy man beseeched our mutual Floridian friend, who opened her golden Rolodex and arranged an immediate surgery.

Thankfully, the procedure was a great success. Before returning to India, my friend in Florida hosted a party for all those who helped Tendral on her journey.

"Wake up. Somebody wants to meet you," Dana whispered to me sweetly on a blindingly bright Florida morning. Half asleep,

I padded across a thick Persian rug into the opulent living room, tying my plush terry-cloth robe around me as I shuffled. Dana held up baby Tendral to meet me. Straight, jet-black hair, poking up every which way, eyes containing the night's sky. My hands instinctively reached under her arms. Lifting her up, taking a giant whiff of her head, I absorbed her perfume the way I'd smell a bouquet of flowers. My knees felt weak as I inhaled the sweetest sugar mixed with warm talcum powder. I was surprised at how solid she was, the substance of a miracle. She lifted her fisted hands over her head like a champion prize fighter as I felt her say, *I've been through hell and back—I'm here for a reason.*

I immediately loved her and felt intoxicated by her presence; a beyond-this-world connection wrapped around my heart like ivy. Her caretakers whispered enthusiastically while I danced with Tendral to our own soul song, lifting her to peer into her smiling, dark eyes. The holy man announced, "She looks like she belongs to you."

Dana and I looked at each other with the telepathic knowing of a couple who has been together for years. Suddenly our infertility, like scattered pieces of a jigsaw puzzle, magnetized into place, and in an instant, our world made perfect sense: without looking for her, we'd found her. Nodding in agreement, Dana and I said a hearty yes to being Tendral's parents.

For the next two weeks, between meetings for our program, we spent as much time with this glorious powerhouse of a soul as we could. I memorized Tendral's beautiful pink lips with uneven, bumpy scars in all the right places, allowing her to devour bottle after bottle, making up for lost time.

A few days before we were scheduled to fly home, I was gripped with a fierce instinct to stay in Florida until the expedited adoption was complete so we could fly Tendral home to L.A. in our arms. But the entire contingent, including the lawyer drawing up the paperwork, instructed Dana and me to go home, get our home prepared for her, and then come back once the legalities reflected what Dana and I already knew in our hearts.

I told Dana I felt an overpowering primal, cavewoman drive to grab Tendral, tuck her into my jacket, and run to the plane, smuggling her back home with us. Dana cautioned me—since we were so close to being her parents—to not make a scene and play it cool so the others wouldn't interpret my passion as unfit behavior to be her mother.

Against the riptide of my intuition, I stuffed my knowing into my suitcase, took deep breaths, wore the mask of a cool, level-headed woman, and forced myself to board the plane, counting the days, hours, minutes when we could return and claim our baby.

A month later, moments before the phone rang, Dana and I were all nerves, having spent thirty days preparing mentally, emotionally, spiritually, physically our family, our entire world, to make room to be joined the next day—Valentine's Day—with our adopted nine-month-old Tibetan daughter.

Hearing the news that Tendral had drowned in my friend's gold-plated bathtub while her distracted caretaker was wrapped up in a cell phone conversation and left the baby alone, Dana and I crumbled on top of each other. On the cold, yellow linoleum kitchen floor at my friend Jo-e's apartment, we huddled together like survivors in a war zone. A cannon of disbelief, fury, and guilt erupted in my chest, mixed with rage at God, at myself, at everyone who had insisted we leave when I had known otherwise.

Dana and I wailed, heaved, and sputtered, tangled in messy tears, interspersed with loud heartbeats finalizing in deafening silence and the blessed numbness of shock.

The next month, like the one before, was a blur—there was a criminal trial for the caregiver, accused of involuntary manslaughter, but she was ultimately released and sent back to India. Our friends held a quiet, private ceremony for Tendral by the ocean, and Dana and I hunkered down at our friend Gini's place in New Mexico to seek solace. We did our own ceremony on the medicine wheel[18] on her property.

The month before had been a chirpy, dancing, happy whirl, but the month following was a tsunami of grief interspersed with gray days spent in the purgatory of numbness. I desperately sifted through my spiritual toolbox, collected piece by piece over the previous twenty years, curated from the best spiritual teachers of our time: Reverend Michael Beckwith, Eckhart Tolle, Deepak Chopra, Don Miguel Ruiz, Byron Katie, and Marianne Williamson. All the teachings that had always worked in the past to repair my emotional/spiritual/psychological bumps and bruises were rendered useless. All the best platitudes were reduced to plastic children's toys trying to hold together the collapsing tower of my well-being— inept for the magnitude of my devastation.

As I walked the red dirt of the New Mexican trails, I reflected on the fact that before Tendral died, most people would have, I dare say, characterized me as an optimist. I'd invested most of my life in cultivating a relationship with God, spirit, and the Universe—and the payoff was I could find the sun peeking out from behind the corner of even the most grumbling thunder cloud. But in the wake of Tendral's death, my connecting vine to the higher realms was severed, leaving me a robotic ghost of my former self, a postapocalyptic zombie limping across a sun-parched earth.

Until one day, about a month later, in the fog that had become my life, I found myself toggling back and forth between watching

Victor Frankl videos online and reading his famous book, *Man's Search for Meaning*, about logotherapy, his brand of psychotherapy derived from observing human behavior as a prisoner in a Nazi concentration camp. I'd known and admired him for decades but hadn't been so impacted by his wisdom until that day. I was particularly moved by this quote:

> For the meaning of life differs from man to man, from day to day and from hour to hour. What matters, therefore, is not the meaning of life in general but rather the specific meaning of a person's life at a given moment.[19]

After several days spent steeping in his wisdom, I found myself arguing with him in my head, *You can't just make up stories about what you want your life to mean. What about "getting real"? Where does reality fit in here?*

Then in a video (as if in response to my questions), he said, "Despair is suffering without meaning. As long as an individual cannot find, cannot see any meaning in his or her [suffering] . . . he or she will certainly be prone to despair and, under certain conditions, to suicide."[20]

In my attempt to understand what he said, I journaled,

> I believe what Victor Frankl is saying is there is no official empirical meaning to any set of incidents. We human beings, whether consciously or unconsciously, assign meaning to everything that happens, every moment of the day. We make up our stories, believe them, and are impacted by them—and our interpretations will either enhance the flame of our life force or snuff it out. With this in mind, when it comes to the big events of our lives, we might as well choose interpretations that uplift, inspire, vindicate, and/or empower us. At the very

least, we ought to steer clear of crafting stories—like I've been doing—that leave us feeling so hopeless we become obsessed with the myriad ways in which to exit the planet at our own hands.

I snapped my journal shut. In the silence that followed, I became glaringly aware that the story I'd made up about Tendral was killing me. Without meaning to, my default narrative not only took Tendral away from me, but took God away as well. I made up that there was either no God, or if there was, he/she/it surely didn't care about me, Dana, or Tendral. And why would I want to live in such a cruel world governed by such a cruel God?

I was dumbstruck by the realization that, yes, I was heartbroken about Tendral dying, and my dreams of being her mother were dashed. But my suffering was not about those things. My suffering was due to the story I'd made up about what happened.

I contemplated the meaning I might choose instead as I hiked along the jagged red rocks. Breathing in the scent of packed earth, pine, and sagey, sun-drenched piñon trees, I climbed up to Gini's medicine wheel. I stood at the center of the clearing, arms outstretched, asking God, the Universe, and any on-duty angel who might lend an ear to help me find a new story for what had happened to Tendral.

Here's how I OGLE'd it:

O: *What is the Offending behavior and/or situation?*

Tendral died. Her caretaker lost vigilance while she was immersed in her phone call. As a result, this precious being drowned, and along with her, my dream of being her mother.

G: *What is Good about that offending behavior and/or situation?*

It felt impossible to find the good in this situation. But, when I eventually became ready to practice what I preached, I assumed the role of the attorney whose job was to find the treasure amid the tragedy. Like Frankl also instructed, I allowed myself to open to a radically new way of seeing what had happened. Nothing came immediately, but in time, a glimmer of hope began shimmering in a distant part of my i-magic-nation, beckoning me toward it. I indulged my dreaming, childlike, storytelling mind, and what unfolded was this: The What-If Tendral Fairytale.

What if Tendral was an angel sent from heaven for just nine months so I could be her mother and Dana could be her father for a short while?

What if we were lucky to have her in our lives and in our hearts for two glorious in-person weeks? Most people don't get to hold an angel for even two minutes, never mind two weeks!

What if, instead of feeling ripped off for not getting her for a lifetime, I could be grateful for the blessing of being with her for the time we had?

What if she had accomplished in her short life what it takes most people a lifetime to do?

What if her double cleft palate was a marker she was already enlightened and couldn't ingest the amnesia most people do when they take the trip from the angelic realm to the human dimension?

What if the angel assigned to send Tendral down the chute from heaven to earth told her, *Shhhhh, don't tell anyone about all the secrets to the Universe?* What if just as she did this, an earthquake rumbled in excitement as Tendral came to earth, causing the well-intentioned angel to whack Tendral's lips too hard, twice. And instead of it stopping Tendral from keeping her wisdom under wraps, it accidently sent her into the realm of the humans with full, 100 percent awareness?

What if Tendral was my special angel?

And what if, going forward, every time I heard the word *tendril* (which didn't used to be often, but after she died, I began hearing it all the time), instead of feeling a pang of loss, the sound of her name could flip a hope switch in me, helping strengthen my personal tendril connection between heaven and earth?

L: *How am I peering into the Looking Glass (mirror)?*

I also get immersed in the task at hand . . . it could've just as easily been me who wasn't watching her in the tub. In fact, I busied myself with my work in L.A., and I wasn't there for her to watch her during her bath. I can't blame anyone. I let myself drown in my sorrow in the weeks following Tendral's passing. Even though I eventually found blessings in the mess, I am not the same naïve person I was before she died. A part of me died with Tendral . . . and a new part of me has arisen.

E: *How will I allow this situation to Elevate me? What Elevated action will I take?*

By the time I hiked back down from the medicine wheel, my new Tendral Tale in tow, the tangerine-and-magenta sky ablaze, my dark cloud had lifted.

With all my might, I hardwired my new story into my brain, overriding all other stories that cast shadows across my mind. I'm grateful to report that today, twelve years later, I can see that my new narrative resurrected me.

Soon after this revelation, I made the decision to funnel my maternal energy toward the young girls and women in my life whom I feel moved to support, including my wonderful stepdaughter. In Tendral's name, I led several service projects in Guatemala and Colombia with teams of young people from around the world, building homes in poverty-stricken areas.[21]

People marveled at how quickly and gracefully I seemed to emerge through the traumatic loss of Tendral. But what they didn't know is that while I was under the auspices of the first knee-jerk story in the throes of my devastation, I felt no grace whatsoever. But the grace that had been there all along was finally felt by me when I opened to a new story . . . a new dream of my conscious creation. My new mythology placed my joy and freedom at its center and gave me back a renewed and more wholistic relationship with God.

Soon after Tendral's passing, I became known as Doctor Dream and sometimes the Nightmare Whisperer. In large part because of what I learned from my Tendral experience, I created a niche empowering people to reframe not just the devastating dreams that come while asleep but the ones we live in the light of day as well. I believe we humans are dreaming all the time. And I've learned, as did Frankl, that there's nothing more important than remembering we have a say in the story/dream we tell about the events that take place in our lives.

We have the free will to frame our dreams and our lives through the lens of tragedy, comedy, triumph, or blessing, and it is done unto us as we believe. We must remember, although we don't always get a say in what shows up on the canvas of our lives, we always get a say in the frame we surround it with. And, as it turns out, the frame makes all the difference.

A few months after my Tendral breakthrough on the medicine wheel in New Mexico, back in Los Angeles, I was having a bumpy day. Under deadline for my book *It's All in Your Dreams*, a melancholy thought of Tendral seeped into my heart, unannounced. Sitting at my desk, I lifted my head from my computer and leaned back, beseeching her to give me a sign.

A ping announcing an incoming email interrupted my prayer. The email was an inquiry from someone asking if I could suggest any Tibetan dream practices. I nearly curtly replied, "No." But I figured that would be rude. Besides, I'm Doctor Dream; I should at least do some quick research and get back to the poor guy. And . . . Tendral was from Tibet . . . hmmm.

I Googled and clicked on the first article that popped up, written by a scholar named Robert Moss. I scanned the article until about halfway down the page the word *tendril* stood out. I rubbed my eyes, thinking I'd gone mad. I took a deep breath and blinked a few times to make sure it wasn't my contact lenses playing tricks on me. They weren't.

Moss described tendril as an advanced-level dream meditation connecting the dreamer in the lucid state from Samsara (the world of duality and suffering inhabited by us mortals) to the Pure Lands (a heavenly state, beyond duality, that we can tap into at any time). But, primarily, the tendril meditation is for strengthening the dream bridge that connects the living with the dead.

What?

I nearly fell on the floor with the potency of this synchronicity. Electrified, I turned my research toward Moss, found his phone number, and called him right then. He, a world-traveling dream expert who rarely is on the ground long enough to have cell service much less answer the phone from an unknown number, picked up my call on the first ring. We dove headfirst into an hour-and-a-half-long conversation about Tendral, both the dream practice and the being. By the time we ended the call, a friendship had been forged, and I swore to never again doubt the reality of life beyond the veil and our ability to participate in it and, thus, be elevated.

Over the twelve years since I knew Tendral's physical form, I've developed a profound relationship with life on the other side of the veil. None of us get out alive . . . and the pain in losing a loved one can feel impossible to live with. Yet the way we learn to live and the stories we craft about our circumstances shape who we are, who we become, and the legacy we leave behind.

Steal My Phone

Colombia

The robbed that smiles steals something from the thief.
OTHELLO, WILLIAM SHAKESPEARE

My team and I had just arrived at the Bogota bus depot on a service trip with our program CHIME IN (The CHange Is ME INternational) with young people from the US learning firsthand the value of sustainability and giving back to those less fortunate. Our ten-person group was excited to be surrounded by the shining faces, delicious coffee, and colorful lifestyle of our South American brothers and sisters.

Like cavemen with torches encircling a fire, we huddled around our travel bags, awaiting a bus to take us to a farm outside of the city. Removing my cripplingly heavy purse, I placed it like the cherry on top of a tall luggage cake, when I felt a tap on my shoulder. I whipped my ponytailed head to the left to see a well-dressed woman asking me for directions. Apologizing for not knowing, I flipped my head back around to see, feel, and know the absence of my purse. In the seconds my eyes had been distracted, the lovely woman's clever cohort must've swiped it right from under the watchful eye of my husband and our group.

The real gut punch was my purse doubled as my computer bag that held not only my passport; my cell phone (my link to the world, my right hand, my constant companion and safety blanket); and nearly one thousand dollars in pesos—our hard-earned spending money supposed to last for the entire trip—but also my laptop, with all manner of full and partially written manuscripts not backed up. I felt stabbed with daggers in my heart.

My group and I spent the remainder of the night begging the police to scan the security footage so we could find the criminals who did this, to no avail.

Over the next thirty days, I had no choice but to surrender to being deviceless. I spasmed through Elisabeth Kübler-Ross's five stages of grief.[22]

1 **Denial:** This can't be happening. I'm sure this is a dream, a result of jetlag. At any moment, the thief will return my purse, or police will find it, and all will be well.

2 **Anger:** What the hell! (Insert all expletives!) I came here to do service work, and this is the thanks I get! How could I be such a naïve do-gooder to let this happen!

3 **Bargaining:** I knew I should've worn my waist pouch and backpack instead of carrying that gargantuan purse. If I'd only held on to it when the lady tapped my shoulder, I'd still have it.

4 **Depression:** I'll never travel or do any goodwill ever again. This is a horror show. I hate life. Where's God? What's the point of any of it?

5 **Acceptance:** OK. This happened. At least I'm with other people who have phones I can borrow if I have a true emergency. At least the thief didn't physically assault me. It could've been worse. I'm lucky I'll be able to buy a new phone, laptop, and purse when I get home in a month. I'll have an adventure without my phone. There must be a reason for this.

When that wasn't enough, I OGLE'd it:

O: *What is the Offending behavior and/or situation?*

Someone stole my purse; my phone, money, passport, all ID, and mostly, my laptop with all my work (not backed up, my bad) were gone. Years of work, poof, gone, done, bye-bye. I was beyond crushed.

G: *What is Good about that offending behavior and/or situation?*

Nothing! OK, I just had to get that out of my system. Time to adopt the job of the ruthless attorney on the hunt for clues as to how this might be a good thing. To do this, I broke it into weeks:

Week one: Living on an eco-friendly farm, learning to make compost toilets, I had a sort of phantom limb syndrome for my devices. Upon arrival at our eco-village treehouse, I marveled at a peach-and-lavender sunset on the distant volcanos. My arm twitched in midair, reaching for a phone no longer there to capture the precious moment. Despite feeling a disappointment that I couldn't join the others in reporting back to friends and family at home via social media, I let go and simply took a photo with my mind's eye and enjoyed the moment . . . what a concept.

Week two: Being the only person without a phone, I started to notice how much everyone else was a slave to their phones. It seemed their devices had become their vices, as my companions were only half-present while eating our zesty avocado-laden meals, the fruit plucked right from the farm we were on. Like kids on a sugar high, they were in a tug-of-war between the beauty of the present moment and the pinball game happening in their brains, eyes darting back and forth from screens to life whizzing past them. I began to feel sparks of strange gratitude for not having a phone to distract me from the richness of the moment.

Week three: By a miracle, I was able to secure a temporary passport, and we traveled from Colombia to Guatemala. I let myself become fully immersed in the culture. Instead of maniacally posing for selfies with the locals and posting them on social media like my cohorts, I was having genuine conversations, truly connecting with the family we were building a home for, learning about the nuances of their culture, marveling at the way they made brightly colored beaded jewelry as they shared with me the legends of their land. Enjoying myself so deeply, I felt sorry for my previous self, the me of three weeks before, someone compelled to document every moment of life, which left her hyperventilating as she hydroplaned on the surface.

Week four: My heart cracked open. Communing with the elders with eyes filled with wisdom, I reveled in profound gratitude at the gift of not having a cell phone to water down the preciousness of my moments with my amazing new friends.

I walked from the mouth of the river with the women of the village, who wore brightly colored dresses. Without a phone in my hand, I was unable to snap photos of them balancing heavy metal pots on their heads, but I gave them a bit of comic relief as I, the big, strong American, struggled to keep up with them as we walked across the fields. I carried the tiniest pot of water on my head, sloshing with each step, while tiny girls half my size, with babies strapped to their backs, carried pots twice as big as the one I struggled not to drop.

Later the women taught me to make tortillas on an open flame, while confiding in me their pain and desires for a better life for their children, and I fell in love . . . with them, the place, and the unfiltered, uninterrupted moment. Then anxiety crept in about returning home to the seductive whirling world of cell phones and laptops; I was afraid I'd lose my new, calm, present self when I got home.

L: *How am I peering into the Looking Glass (mirror)?*

Maybe it was me (my higher self) who stole my phone from me, so I wouldn't have so many precious moments stolen by being only partially present—as is often the case when living life through our devices.

Every time I multitask, I steal my presence away from the present moment, from the person or people I'm with. By trying to spread myself too thin, I'm the thief who steals precious time from myself that I can't get back.

E: *How will I allow this situation to Elevate me? What Elevated action will I take?*

Back home, I'd like to say I swore off my devices and wrote this story with a quill and sent it via carrier pigeon. But, alas, within a week of being back to city life, I purchased replacement gadgets. I had writing deadlines and work to attend to, after all.

Although I must admit, even though I went back to being a cell phone–carrying Los Angelino, I like to think that because of this situation, I have my phone, but it no longer has me. For example, I don't turn on my phone until about noon each day. It's shut off during meals and after dinner. Throughout the day when I'm writing or spending time with a friend, I put my phone on airplane and do-not-disturb mode.

Four years later, I squirmed in my seat as I watched the 2020 documentary about social media and the tech world, *The Social Dilemma*. In the movie, former heads of Google, Facebook, Pinterest, and YouTube pulled back the curtain on the manipulation behind the scenes of our screens. I also strangely felt smug because when my purse was stolen, I was ejected from the matrix of the cell-phone-attached-at-the-hip life I'd been living and created a buffer—slight though it may have been—between my phone and me.

The most shocking part of the movie was when the geniuses who created the algorithms designed to hook us via pyrotechnic dopamine surges to the brain (in the same way slot machines make the ding sound to stimulate us to shell out more quarters) admitted to forbidding their own children from having phones or from using the apps they'd created.[23]

I know everyone can't be as lucky as I to have been robbed and rendered a Luddite for thirty days. But I hope you'll learn from me not only how to avoid getting your belongings stolen while traveling but how to solve the social dilemma by taking these deliberate steps:

1   Turn off as many notifications as you can live without (I suggest all of them).

2   Make do-not-disturb your friend, especially while you're with actual friends.

3   Repeat this mantra throughout the day: I have a phone, but my phone doesn't have me!

If you can't take heed of my suggestions, then go to your local bus/train station and leave your purse carelessly teetering atop your luggage, with your phone in plain sight. When someone asks you for directions, engage them in conversation and pray a clever thief steals the device that has become your vice.

One Hot Flash
at a Time

Southern California

I'm what is known as perimenopausal.
"Peri," some of you may know, is a Latin prefix meaning
"SHUT YOUR FLIPPIN' PIE HOLE."

CELIA RIVENBARK

Perusing the corrections my editor sent me on my book *Luminous Humanness*, I read a blood-red note in the column where she dared ask, "Could you replace *fanfare* with a more contemporary word, like *drama*?"

Aw, fiddlesticks! I must seem like an old lady to that little whippersnapper!

Shit! Only an old lady would say fiddlesticks or call a millennial a whippersnapper!

I cursed as my entire body, in a flash, turned from winter to summer.

To my credit, *fanfare*, *fiddlesticks*, and *whippersnapper* aren't words from my Gen-X era. I'm a fifty-four-year-old who still thinks she can get away with shopping at Forever 21 (even though I don't anymore due to speculation about child labor). I borrowed those old-fogey expressions from my grandparents, who lived through the Great Depression. Years ago, I started using those words in an attempt to be funny, and they stuck, becoming part of my vernacular.

Guilty as charged, damn millennial! I thought as my ego blazed crimson.

I don't know if this is the case for anyone but me, but it seems my hot flashes are triggered by shame and even from her shy cousin, embarrassment. All I know is when a hot flash comes over me, I feel like I'm before a police squad shining an accusatory overhead interrogation light, catching me red-handed with the loot, red-faced, pants down, busted.

The heat bursts first in my cheeks, then radiates through my chest, blazing down my arms, erupting into my stomach, until I'm a full-body blush, glistening in a layer of sweat, twenty degrees hotter than I'd been just moments before.

The late, great contemporary of my grandparents, Margaret Meade, said we should be anthropologists of our lives. I'm one-upping her, as a precocious youngster should, and I do my darndest (another grandparent word) to be the detective of my life. Peering with a magnifying glass beneath the surface, I observed my little hotties were like electric fence shocks to my system, jolting me into awareness that I'm indulging in stinking thinking, like *Kelly, you are not prepared enough, you don't know enough, you didn't do enough, and basically, you aren't enough.*

My inner Nancy Drew (the likes of whom, I'm sure, my millennial editor has never heard of) observed that even while sleeping, I get hot and bothered (not in a sexy way), awakening sweating after having had a shaming dream.

Enough! It was time to OGLE my hot flashes!

Here's how I OGLE'd it:

O: *What is the Offending behavior and/or situation?*

Damn hot flashes, a result of out-of-whack hormones, turning my internal ecosystem from Iceland to Panama in the blink of an eye. They awaken me in the night, keeping me from getting a good night's sleep (and how am I supposed to dream if I can't sleep—and I'm Doctor Dream, for Christ's sake!).

G: *What is Good about that offending behavior and/or situation?*

What if my hot flashes are biological news flashes, trying to wake me up to where I think I'm not measuring up? Maybe what's good about them is they are an internal alarm system alerting me when my thoughts have veered off track.

L: *How am I peering into the Looking Glass (mirror)?*

What if these scalding jolts, more than just the result of a hormone imbalance, are my higher self sending a message—like pain that comes from touching a hot stove—alerting me to drop my stinking thinking like it's hot . . . because it is.

E: *How will I allow this situation to Elevate me? What Elevated action will I take?*

I shared my observations with a dear friend, Ruble, who suggested that every time I notice a shame-inducing hot flash, I wrap myself in a cold compress of self forgiveness and envision my inner mother and father comforting me by saying: *You are wonderful despite having made mistakes. I expect a lot of you and hold you to a high standard. But don't worry, you're not in trouble. I see you trying. You're safe. I love you.*

PS: My actual mother and father would say those things to me, if asked. What's attempting to be transformed here is my inner taskmaster with white gloves, doctor's lab coat, whips, nose in the air, just waiting for the opportunity to toss me off the island for making the slightest infraction.

So, now when I get a hot flash, I immediately fire affirmations back at my inner Cruella and, thus, drown out her critical voice yelling at me, "You're not enough!" If I keep this up, I'll become the queen of self-love in the process, and I just might render my hot flashes out of a job. Or maybe these heat-orgasms, as my friend Jenni Murphy likes to call them, could get a promotion and begin alerting me to higher-caliber thoughts or behaviors.

Or if my scalding surges find no better use, perhaps they will simply slip quietly into retirement, like a decorated war veteran, in a blaze of glory, feeling proud for having done a noble job.

Armed with this awareness, my hot flashes melted like the Wicked Witch of the West in an ice bucket challenge. I girded my loins to read the next critical comment from my cruel young'un editor. Only, upon closer examination, I realized it wasn't criticism at all. Her next blood-red note enthusiastically read, "Love this!" as she highlighted this paragraph:

November 16th

You Are De-Light

Be delighted by your own process in the way a parent is enthralled by their child's first step, first tooth, or first words. See yourself from the vantage point of a loving mother who knows the areas of life you most struggle with are the areas you deserve the most love, kindness, and compassion. Feel your inner father wrap his arms around you when you fumble, coo at you when you bumble and pick you up when you stumble.[24]

I felt encouraged by my millennial editor's appreciation of my writing—maybe my snap judgment about her was too harsh. She's kind of brilliant, for a whippersnapper. Now that my period has left without saying goodbye, I'm finding myself feeling nostalgic. I realized what had been sorely missing in my life: a role model to see me through this rite of passage like I had back in the summer of 1980, when I started my period at twelve years old and turned to Judy

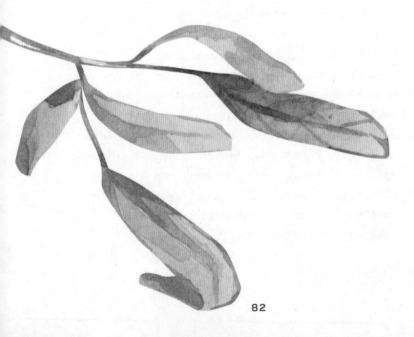

Blume's Margaret from *Are You There, God? It's Me, Margaret* (another character I assume is lost on my young editor), whose journey made me feel excited about getting my period.[25]

Dear Ms. Blume,

It's me, Kelly.
Can you please write a story about what happens to Margaret when her period goes away?
Was God there to help her through her awkward transition?
When Margaret lost her period, gained weight, and had hot flashes, did she find the energy to flounce hand in hand into the sunset with the salt-and-pepper-haired guy of her dreams?

In my attempt to not just go through the change but be the change I wished to see in the world, I thought I'd dedicate this Kelly Clarkson–inspired lyric to my period: "Since you've been gone, all I have are my hot flashes to keep me warm."

With my torch song and my new self-love regimen in place, my hot flashes may soon be gone as well. I've never been one for goodbyes, and never been much of a fan of periods, the bloody ones that soiled my panties or the ones that punctuate the end of sentences— they're both so permanent, after all—but I'll try to reconcile:

Sayonara, period, thanks for the good times, the embarrassing times, and the messy and oh-so-inconvenient times. I love you and can't say I'll miss you. But don't worry, you're not in trouble. You are safe, and I love you, period.

When the Ambulance Blared for Me

Southern California

He who binds to himself a joy
Does the winged life destroy
But he who kisses the joy as it flies
Lives in eternity's sunrise.

WILLIAM BLAKE

When I hear a high-pitched shrill of an ambulance blur by me on the street, I recoil and feel startled, anxious, concerned. My Catholic background kicks in, moving my right hand involuntarily into the sign of the cross: center finger to my forehead, then to my chest, to the left side of my chest, followed by a tap on the right side of my chest. As I touch my lips, I send out a silent prayer for the injured, *God help them.*

But on the evening the siren blared for me, I didn't see the red trucks, stretcher, oxygen mask, nor did I hear the gasping of the crowd in the Indian restaurant on the hot summer night. In fact, the anxiety that had been building within me for days had curiously vanished.

Just an hour before the pandemonium, Dana and I joined our two dear friends Ron and Moira to celebrate my fortieth birthday. I chose our favorite spot, the Gate of India, for saag paneer, garlic naan, and mango lassis, a block from the bright lights and pulsating music of the 3rd Street Promenade in Santa Monica, California, near where we live. I tasted the salty air of the Pacific Ocean on my lips and knew it would be a magical night.

Hungrily awaiting the arrival of our savory food, Moira, a world-class vegan chef, removed a chunky chocolate chip cookie in a Ziplock bag from her purse. "Since tonight's a special occasion, let's have dessert before our meal," she announced as she divided the glorious delight into four pieces on a bright-gold napkin. Ravenous from barely eating that day, I reached in, grabbed the thumb-size crumbly piece closest to me, and gobbled it. As it melted in my happy mouth, Moira cautioned, "I should've warned you—this is one of my special cookies."

Everything Moira touches turns delicious. I'd always enjoyed her culinary artistry. But until then, I'd only heard about her special cookies—sprinkled with nutmeg, cinnamon, and a pinch of hash— that might make you high. I'd never had one before that night, but I thought they sounded harmless. Come on, an innocent dessert can't possibly make you wonky. I scanned myself for any strange sensations incited by the morsel and shrugged, thinking, *I don't feel any different.*

As I savored each decadent bite of the sweet-and-spicy cuisine, I also soaked up every dollop of lively conversation, zestier than dinner. Eventually, our plates emptied, and the button on my pants tried to make a spring-loaded getaway. Then, without warning, the room began to spin. Orange-and-yellow-sequined tapestry became blindingly bright and splotchy as the scent of curry burned my nostrils. Whirling words and laughter became a slow-motion, surround-sound, not-so-merry-go-round spinning progressively faster and faster.

Panicking in response to the parade stampeding my brain, I felt like a juggler with more balls in the air than she could catch. Just beneath the flurry of a thousand butterfly wings flapping in my chest, I realized I was losing my grip. Veiling a kaleidoscope of color, it was as if a black blindfold slipped over my eyes. My will to fight deserted me, leaving me with no choice but surrender.

My friends thought I was being lovey-dovey with Dana when my head fell to his shoulder, with my eyes closed and face turned away from their banter. They didn't realize I was no longer there. Afraid for my life, I began chanting the only prayer I could muster, "God, God, God . . ."

I don't know how, but this desperate plea seemed to propel me through a cosmic birth canal. Once I popped out the other side, I was flung like a pebble from a slingshot across time and space into the center of the aurora borealis . . . free . . . light . . . expansive . . . Then I slipped away. Life as I knew it was over. Relieved, I gratefully floated up.

Eventually, as I was later told, Dana and our friends realized something was wrong when I didn't respond to the conversation. They poked at me, then yelled at me to get my attention. Dana even shook me. Seeing my face had become pale and cold, he sprung into a full-blown panic. Moira yelled at the waiter to call 9-1-1, while Ron threw his ice water on me, to no avail. I remained unresponsive because I wasn't in my body.

The floodgates opened; no longer in charge, I was on the ride, going where it—whatever it was—wanted to take me. I was without a body but aware I was still me. I had my thoughts, my perspective, internal commentary, but I was liberated—at one with the swirling rainbow light show of the Universe.

Just moments before, I'd been confined to an ego prison inside an earthbound body, white knuckles grasping the guide rails of my life in response to the stress associated with the stock market crash of 2008.

We were in the process of downsizing from our home in the Hollywood Hills, and worry had become my norm. But I was suddenly freed from my shackles, elevated beyond the myopia of my tiny world to a viewpoint that contained the vastness of the sky.

Without the density of my body, I could suddenly soar through the universe—weightless, timeless, enormous, *whooooooooooosh*. I didn't *feel* love; I *was* love—an entire ocean of it. All separation and suffering dissolved like a wave toppling over a sandcastle, blending everything into oneness.

Rising from glory to greater glory, I realized there was no end to love, no ceiling and no walls. Just when I thought it couldn't possibly get any better, there was more—eternities more—like thick honey pouring itself through my awareness in a never-ending expanse of bliss.

I was filled with the absolute knowing that my struggles on earth were ridiculous, for I am and always have been (just as we all are) more than a little teacup container. From my sudden big-picture perspective, I knew it was possible to treat life like the great adventure it truly is. I realized with 100 percent certainty life is a wonderful dream, where it's possible to savor every moment, relationship, sunset, kiss, accomplishment, and struggle—even amid financial distress, heartbreaks, and natural and unnatural disasters. Then, when the time is right, I can let it all go, freely moving on, without grief, toward the next magnificent horizon.

I began to be aware of the commotion going on in the restaurant and around my body, tugging at me. I felt the urgency to reassure my companions I was OK—more than OK . . . in full-blown bliss. But they could not find my wavelength or receive my earnest attempts at telepathic communication. I felt guilty for having the time of my life while my husband and friends were in distress. Despite the heaven I was experiencing, my need for them to be OK took over as I willed my spirit back into my body. This was not an easy feat. It was like trying to fit the entire sky into a tiny teacup.

After what seemed a lifetime (about fifteen minutes in earth time), I found myself on the sidewalk outside the restaurant. On a gurney, with an oxygen mask over my mouth, I was about to be loaded into an ambulance.

Back in my body, I grabbed the tan, muscled arm of the paramedic to my left and directed in a robotic voice, "Check my pulse. I'm back. No need to waste a perfectly good ambulance." Sure enough, my vital signs reemerged, and I gazed upon my teary husband and worried friends, saying, "Hey, guys, what's all the fuss about? Death is awesome! Or more accurately, life without the body is glorious, and lo and behold, it's still life!"

Here's how I OGLE'd it:

O: *What is the Offending behavior and/or situation?*

Leaving my body. Dying, as it turns out, is the ultimate offense—one that, literally, threatens not just our ability to thrive but survive. Oh yes, and this experience scared the bejesus out of my husband.

By the way, because many people have asked, no, I don't have a medical condition, although I have been prone to anemia and low blood sugar. But in this instance, because I'm a "lightweight" when it comes to recreational drugs (or any kind for that matter), I had an extreme reaction that took me way beyond the "high" that was intended.

G: *What is Good about that offending behavior and/or situation?*

Because of what happened, I now know even the worst thing isn't so bad—in fact, once I surrendered, it was the most extraordinary experience of my life. Had I not been gifted with the realization that I am not my body, I might be more attached than I am now.

I'd had many glimpses of the heavenly realms over the four decades before this experience via meditation, dreams, prayers, dance, yoga, and visions but none quite as extensive and immersive as this. I later discovered an experience like this is similar to the phenomenon of a high-potency dream. Instead of its energy dissipating over time, it gains intensity, and its message progresses the more we contemplate it.

L: *How am I peering into the Looking Glass (mirror)?*

One of the things I avoid and treat like the plague is endings, as if to say just because something exists or is good or has some inherent value, it should live forever. But perhaps there is a wiser part of me that set me up with this death experience to have a visceral, personal experience with impermanence and discover it is (and can be) the most liberating thing there is. Maybe I created (or at least cocreated) this situation to become a freer version of myself.

E: *How will I allow this situation to Elevate me? What Elevated action will I take?*

Don't get me wrong; I love having a body and being a part of this world. And I want to continue, as long as my physical form can healthfully do so. But when it's time to go or time for my loved ones to shuffle off this mortal coil, I intend to make transitions as much of a celebratory graduation party as possible.

Soon after this experience, I ran into Dannion Brinkley at a mind/body/spirit type of conference. He's the *New York Times* best-selling author of *Saved by the Light*. Dannion is famous for dying four times and returning to tell the tales and is known affectionately as Dr. Death. Curious as to what his opinion would be of my experience, I asked him how such a small bite of a special cookie could send me over the edge.

He responded in his inimitable Southern drawl, "Your guides must have wanted to show you somethin'. Those little buggers found a window of opportunity, and they nabbed you. It wasn't your time to go, so they let you come back. If you're smart, you'll take in the message you received, integrate it into your life, and share it with others. It is a gift when this happens. It can change your life."[26]

13

Overbearing

Southern California

No one can make you feel inferior without your consent.

ELEANOR ROOSEVELT

I couldn't wait to meet the world-renowned psychic my writing teacher had been telling the class about. "She's incredible," my teacher assured us. "She'll read your energy like a book—ha ha—and her insights will give you a window into how to become a better writer."

I was always game for a psychic reading, a fresh aha moment, a hopeful glimmer about successful things to come.

My classmates and I awaited the psychic's arrival in my teacher's shabby-chic Malibu living room, overlooking the blue and green of the Pacific Ocean. The eight of us sat encircled in overstuffed plush chairs, sipping chai, breathing in jasmine-scented candles, wiggling like kids hopped up on too many candy canes, squirming in line, waiting our turn to sit on Santa's lap.

Then a patchouli breeze wafted through the room as she floated in—a statuesque, aloof queen with a crown of hair piled high. Her white gossamer robe flowed behind her like a wedding dress. The psychic took her seat and instructed us to close our eyes and take a few deep breaths. She then led us on a meditative journey, to tap into our true essence.

I followed her instructions to the letter as I nestled into a blissful pocket of peace. I could feel her penetrating gaze—scanning my energy, assessing the nature of my soul. Aware I was being evaluated, the people pleaser in me sat upright, donning my best spiritual behavior, picturing a bright light emanating from my heart to hers. I thought it couldn't hurt my chances of getting a more favorable reading. That's how I spent the next thirty minutes, beaming wave after wave of love to her.

When the meditation was over, she gazed at each student for several minutes, like an anthropologist, peering beyond protective layers directly into their souls. During the pregnant pause, we all held our breath in anticipation of her utterance of a single word that would describe each person's true nature.

To my friend Jo-e, the psychic teared up, placing her hand over her heart, as she simply said, "Wise."

Ahhh, I thought, *this woman's right on*. Jo-e is the wisest person I know.

Then she moved the spotlight of her attention to Mike, a gifted writer with a wounded past and clever turn of phrase, and said in her breathy tone, "Brilliant."

"Damn, she's good," I heard myself say. Mike is totally brilliant.

She moved on to the other members of our group, assessing them as, "Powerful, generous, intuitive . . ."

I thought, *She's so perceptive at identifying the soul essence of my class-mates.* I couldn't wait to hear what she'd say about me. Then finally, the moment came. She took a long look in my eyes, and with her voice like a spring breeze, she uttered, "Overbearing."

I cocked my head to the side like a dog hearing an ambulance siren.

What? I thought but said nothing out loud. I was sure I had heard her incorrectly.

I smiled and giggled, trying to play it off like it was a joke, thinking, *Ha ha, very funny, lady. . . . What's my real word?*

Instead of giving me a new word or even laughing at her hilarious joke, in a serious tone, not batting an eyelash, she moved on to the next student and the next. "Sweetness, peaceful . . ."

But all I could hear was the word *overbearing* repeating in time with my heartbeat drumming in my ears.

WTF! I seethed in my inner voice. I looked around at the rest of the class to see if they had heard the same thing I did . . . and to see if anyone was going to jump to my defense. But, alas, everyone continued steeping in the meditative trance this charlatan had cast.

I excused myself to the opulent bathroom and paced back and forth. How could it be no one else thought there was anything wrong with this situation? *This is ridiculous!* I thought. *Over-freaking-bearing, my ass! Me? WTF. Bullshit! I demand a do-over. Clearly this woman has no idea who I really am. I reject this so-called psychic reading completely.*

I wanted to slam the door, stomp through the room, grab my belongings, and leave in a huff, but that would just prove her right. Ha! If I was truly overbearing, I would've told her off right then and there. So, I did what someone with a calm, sweet soul would do, and I stewed in my thoughts while counting the minutes for this ordeal to be over.

I left class feeling numb, kicked in the belly, invalidated. I thought about the people in my life I'd labeled as overbearing: people who talk over everyone, leaving me feeling like a vampire had guzzled my life force. *They suck! There's no way I'm like them! I am not overbearing; I am as gentle as a lamb! I'm a freaking flower flowing in the breeze, more vulnerable, sweet, and kind than all those assholes.* Damn! OK, maybe I was not as gentle as I thought.

Here's how I (eventually) OGLE'd it:

O: *What is the Offending behavior and/or situation?*

That "psychic" dared to call me—delicate little me—overbearing. It hurt my feelings . . . and felt rude and untrue.

G: *What is Good about that offending behavior and/or situation?*

It's important to label things and people—it has its place. If there was gold here, it was in disguise. Maybe this was something in my blind spot, and it was high time I embraced this aspect of myself.

What's good about being called overbearing? At first, I could think of absolutely nothing. But, as I gestated, I realized overbearing is akin to confidence, boldness, self-expression, an enthusiastic participation in life. Perhaps *overbearing*, like any shadow (according to the late Debbie Ford, author of one of my favorite books, *The Dark Side of the Light Chasers*), is a good, life-enhancing quality, just turned up a notch or two or three too high.

L: *How am I peering into the Looking Glass (mirror)?*

Just like the psychic, I've judged people at first blush, only to find out, upon getting to know them better, there was (way) more to the story beneath the surface.

In dreams, I'm fond of saying (to other people) that everyone and everything in the dream is the dreamer. So, could it be in this waking dream, the psychic was the part of me who was trying to make me aware of this blind spot?

Yikes. I certainly don't mean to be overbearing... and never, ever intend to be a bull in anyone's china shop, stepping on toes and inserting myself in a way that leaves people feeling smashed. And then the movie reel began to play, my life review in fast-forward, as if under a time-lapse lens. ... At first it showed me how as a child I was paralyzingly shy with strangers, closing my eyes, balling my hands into tight fists, wishing people away. Then, in fifth grade, I fainted when I had to stand in front of the class and give an oral report. The following year, in response to getting terribly bullied in junior high, I developed a protective shield that feigned fearlessness so as to not give the mean girls the satisfaction of knowing they'd hurt me. This compensation mechanism, my haughty attitude, saved me from getting beaten up. It was like an overzealous bodyguard on too much Red Bull who helped me throughout my life, especially when I felt the most insecure. She overcompensated for my jittery not-enough-ness by puffing me up, so I wouldn't have to feel the fiery pokers of pain.

I remembered what I learned about shadow work and how our vulnerability is loveable, but our defense mechanisms are what get us into trouble—even though the defense mechanisms were born during a time when our vulnerability felt like a liability. Sheesh! Sometimes being human can feel like playing tag with blinders on, through a minefield.

And then, pops of memory flashed back to the times when . . .

- My friend Ron said he'd never sit through a movie with me because I "listen too loudly," unknowingly making boisterous "Ooohs" and "Ahhs" in time with the action on the screen.

- Another friend pointed out how, on my radio show, I always have to have the final word, even after my guests have a mic-drop moment.

- A cofacilitator on a social-service project couldn't stop laughing when I mentioned I thought I should work on being more assertive.

- Even my husband, all the times he made Leo (my astrological sign) wisecracks about how I take over in social situations.

E: *How will I allow this situation to Elevate me? What Elevated action will I take?*

At last, as the saying goes, "Tragedy plus time equals comedy." I can finally laugh at this situation and see the blessing in it. Because of this incident, these days I check in with the people closest to me and ask them if I'm being overly overbearing. Even when I think I'm being Lionel Richie, easy as a Sunday morning, I remember I'm always being some version of intense, even while sleeping, dreaming, or meditating. Now *that's* a skill.

Today, fourteen years later, I'm grateful this incident happened; throughout each day I check myself to see if my assertive behavior is emanating from a still place of true inner peace and divine guidance or if it's masking fear. If I can feel the jitters (a telltale sign fear is in the house), then I do my inner work to shine light on the unease until it dissolves. Then the me beneath the surface can come out to play, like the golden Buddha minus the layers of clay (more on this later, on page 244).

All I do know, as a result of this meeting with the psychic, is I no longer easily hand my faith over to those who claim to know better than I about the state of my soul. Not to say I'm not available to the insights of qualified experts, from time to time. But these days, I first attune to my own higher guidance, who is much more qualified to be the bearer of insight into what I need to know for my soul's journey.

Oh yes, did this meeting with the psychic contribute to me becoming a better writer?

Hell no. Absolutely not.

OK, well, maybe.

Perhaps everything that triggers self-reflection makes us better, more-aware people, but I'll never give her the satisfaction of knowing that. I don't know how my overbearingness shows up in my writing, but in this book, I wouldn't be surprised if I get accused of over*sharing*.

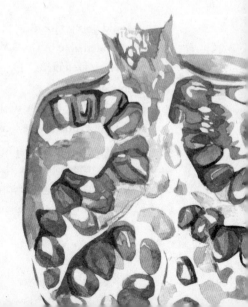

Searching for Satya

Southern California

> *I find it wholesome to be alone the greater part of the time.*
> *To be in company, even with the best, is soon wearisome and*
> *dissipating. I love to be alone. I never found the companion*
> *that was so companionable as solitude.*
>
> HENRY DAVID THOREAU

"Why would you go looking for a missing person that not even the police have been able to find? You're Doctor Dream, for God's sake, not the Dream Detective!" Dana beseeched, scratching his head.

He was right.

We had enough drama with our family as it was without me spending time I didn't have looking for a young woman who'd been missing from my neighborhood for nine years. Even in the best-case scenario, the fact that she'd been gone for so long probably meant she didn't want to be found. But I'm getting ahead of myself (again). . . . Here's what happened the day before . . .

I was jogging through the state park near my house when I ran by my neighbor Sharon. We had the same workout timing: dusk, when the summer air was cooling the canyon. Normally we'd just exchange pleasantries, but on this day, she hollered, "I hear you're into dreams. I have vivid ones . . . about my daughter."

Slowing my jog slightly, not in social-butterfly mode at all as I was on a mission to get in my workout before sunset, I quipped over my shoulder, "Oh, cool."

She replied, "My daughter, Tess, has been missing for nine years. Everyone thinks she's dead, but in my dream, she's still alive."

What?

I screeched to a halt, causing the pinkish dust beneath my feet to plume, as my body joined paces with hers. Ditching my workout plans, I removed my earbuds to let this relative stranger fill my ears with the tragic tale of her daughter.

"Tess was twenty-nine when she went missing on November 17, 2012. She lived here [in Topanga] but was last seen in Capitola Beach near Santa Cruz. If she's still alive, she'd be thirty-eight. Her car was found nine years ago with no sign of foul play, with her earthly belongings intact: clothing, wallet, money, keys, cell phone, groceries . . . everything but her blue ukulele, her most cherished possession."

We stopped. As the sun set on the canyon, she continued, "Over the years I've hired psychics, detectives, and psychic detectives, to no avail. My family believes Tess is dead . . . they're all wanting a memorial service so we can have closure. But these dreams I have of her feel so real. In fact, in my dreams, she goes by the name Satya, which I looked up and discovered means *truth* in Sanskrit."

As Sharon and I continued hiking along the darkening red rocks, past caves and around roots poking out from beneath the dusty path, Sharon told me Tess's favorite movie was *Into the Wild*, a true story about a young man who left his car full of worldly possessions and ventured alone into the woods. She described her daughter as talented, creative, spiritual, sensitive—maybe too sensitive for this world—emotionally erratic, nomadic, never keeping a job or a home for long, and often saying, "I don't belong here . . . this world is not my home."

I asked Sharon if she'd ever heard of true-crime podcasts. "Maybe one of them could help find your daughter," I said, reaching for straws, desperate to be helpful. "These shows open cold cases to the public...and in some instances, missing people get found."

"How could I get on one of those podcasts?" Sharon asked with a hopeful spark.

I heard myself stammer, my mouth running away. "Well . . . I . . . have a podcast. Mine's a mind/body/spirit/dream show—not true crime—but I also have family members in the police and investigation business . . . and because of my show, I have access to the world's best healers and psychics. Maybe I can rally the troops to see if they can help . . ."

That night I told Dana all about my conversation with Sharon. This was when he interrogated me about why on earth I'd thought I could suddenly transform my *Ask Doctor Dream* podcast (now called the *Kelly Sullivan Walden Show*) into a true-crime show.

I rolled my eyes and said, "Since when do I ever do anything that makes sense? Let me sleep on it and see what my dreams have to say about whether I should do this."

That night I dreamed: I'm having breakfast with a dark-haired woman (maybe Tess or Satya). The waitress serves my breakfast, a platter of pink, heart-shaped, frosty cupcakes. *Lovely,* I think, *but this is too much sugar for breakfast.*

Then the waitress brings the dark-haired woman eggs with broken yolks, with a side dish of a tiny, living unicorn. I gasp. *I want what she's having.*

Upon awakening, I interpreted the broken eggs as the tragic aspect of the situation with Tess/Satya, being un-yoked from her family. The unicorn symbolized there could be magic involved (even if only as a side). And maybe she was the unicorn? All I knew was I felt this dream was a sign, giving me the impetus to embark on this nitty-gritty journey, while being on the lookout for the magic amid the tragic.

I immediately called my sister, Tawni, a Veronica Lake–look-alike private eye straight out of a film noir movie, and she jumped on the case. A few days later, Sharon invited me to her house to go through boxes of Tess/Satya's writing, including a book of original poetry entitled *Crying in Public* and a song called "Where You Belong."

A few weeks later, I took the leap into the mystery and started episode one of a special series within my *Ask Doctor Dream* show, titled "Searching for Satya—Calling All Dreamers." My second episode featured a world-renowned healer, Judy Wilkens-Smith, a constellation therapist who said that the family member who acts out the most is often the one who's volunteered to carry unresolved trauma from the family line, so the rest of the family doesn't have to.[27]

Off-air, Judy had asked Sharon about any trauma she knew of in her lineage. She revealed that both sets of Tess's grandparents survived the Holocaust. In fact, Tess was originally going to be named Elsa, after her paternal grandmother, who survived Nazi concentration camps.

Wilkens-Smith said the family owes Tess/Satya a debt of gratitude for taking on the trauma of these unthinkably painful ancestral wounds so it wouldn't be necessary for others to experience the same pain.

In the following episodes, in addition to meeting with the police who had been a part of her case, I interviewed other family members and Elias Lonsdale, an astrologer who had conducted a dozen sessions with Tess/Satya, including one of the last calls before she went missing.

Two months into my investigation I made a list of the theories posed about what might've happened to Tess/Satya:

1   Murder

2   Abduction

3   In a cult

4   Homeless

5   A walk-in (another soul took over her body)

6   Inspired by the movie *Into the Wild*, living in the woods

7   Taken by aliens

Episode seven brought a shock from the Palm Springs psychic medium Timothy Courtney. Courtney has a successful track record working with the police finding missing people. I brought him in to do a psychic reading, but very quickly his gifts for mediumship kicked in when he realized he was communicating with Tess/Satya on the other side. In his vision, he saw she had been abducted and murdered nine years before, soon after she went missing. He described the gruesome details of her struggle and ultimate drowning, but that from the moment of her death, she'd been home . . . in her true home . . . no longer suffering. He said (and I paraphrase), "Tess/Satya is sorry to have caused you and your family so much heartache." Your dreams about her are her showing you she's still alive, not physically but spiritually.[28]

Despite this being devastating news for Sharon (and all who'd been involved in the case), there was also a strange peace that rippled through Sharon to all of us. She later told me that even though she'd never give up looking for her daughter, the thought that her daughter wasn't suffering, nor had she been avoiding her all these years, lifted a heavy weight from her shoulders that enabled her to breathe better.

A couple of days later, Sharon received an urgent voice mail from Elias Lonsdale, the astrologer, who had no idea about Courtney's psychic reading. Lonsdale shared that his wife, who'd never met Tess/Satya, had just awoken from a vivid dream. In her dream, she was shopping at the farmers' market and was introduced to Tess, a petite woman with long, dark hair who said, "I don't go by the name Tess any longer. I go by the name Elsa."[29] There was a feeling in the dream that she had been through quite a journey, and Elsa said that she had found her home, that she was at last at home.

Lonsdale's wife said the girl became flooded with the most extraordinary light . . . that was still visible filling their house even after she woke up.

Sharon broke down in tears. No one but Sharon and her ex-husband knew Tess was going to be named Elsa. Tess had now claimed the name of her brave matriarch, and in so doing, gave her mother, Sharon, the final confirmation she needed to call a family meeting to discuss, after nine long, hard years, a memorial service—a service for not only Tess but also Elsa, and the rest of the family, who had been long overdue for a proper honoring.

Here's how I OGLE'd it:

O: *What is the Offending behavior and/or situation?*

Tess went missing, without a trace, and left her family in a purgatory limbo, unable to grieve their loss.

G: *What is Good about that offending behavior and/or situation?*

It's brave to break out of the collective domestication of our world and claim a new path for oneself, even though it can be dangerous and frightening. It's also what Henry David Thoreau (one of Tess's favorite authors) wrote about in his most famous book (also a favorite of mine, not just because of my last name), *Walden*—the virtues of breaking ties with the trappings of conventional society. If it wasn't for Tess/Elsa's disappearance, I never would've created this podcast series—one that many listeners told me impacted them, either because they related to Tess or because they'd been ghosted by a loved one or were grappling with unresolved issues with someone on the other side.

L: *How am I peering into the Looking Glass (mirror)?*

I, too, have a strong wanderlust part of me that dreams of being completely untethered ... of walking unencumbered through this world, dancing to the beat of my own rhythm. This part of me also knows my true home isn't in this world but in my heavenly king-queendom.

E: *How will I allow this situation to Elevate me? What Elevated action will I take?*

By getting to know the wildly emotional Tess/Satya/Elsa part of me during this time, I was able to pay homage to the women in my lineage upon whose shoulders I stand. Because of this experience, I feel more emboldened to take risks, spend time alone in nature, and follow where my soul guides me (while making sure to intermittently check in with the people who might worry about me). I also feel even more inspired about the realm of dreams. This whole experience was bookended by dreams, starting with Sharon stopping me in my tracks and telling me about her nighttime visits from Tess, then with this final dream confirmation by Elias Lonsdale's wife. Oh yes, and I can't forget my unicorn dream, which proved to be true: it was tragic, but ultimately, there was a heaping side dish of magic . . . and sometimes, the side dish is why we order the meal.

15

Mosaic [30]

Florida

We are mosaics. Pieces of light, love, history, stars . . .
Glued together with magic and music and words.

ANITA KRIZZAN

It was after midnight a few days after Thanksgiving, and a handsome young tennis pro, Brian Newcomer, was on the road heading to work. He was going to drop off his girlfriend, Jessica, along the way. Earlier that night the two of them celebrated their new commitment to each other and their exciting plans. They were the loves of each other's lives. The happy couple marveled at how lucky they

were, and how one great experience seemed to keep leading to the next, and to the next . . .

Then, with no warning, Brian's car motor suddenly began to sputter and slowed to a stop in the middle of the freeway . . . between off ramps . . . with no shoulder available on which to pull over. They were hit from behind, instantly killing Brian, age twenty-seven, and seriously injuring Jessica.

Several days later, Brian's sister Katherine, a former housemate of mine, called. Through sobs she delivered the devastating news. Over the years Katherine had shared stories about Brian, and even though I'd never met him, I felt I knew him. At the end of our call, she asked if I would be willing to provide therapy for her family.

I told her I would be honored to support her and her family in any way I could. Before I knew it, Brian's family had booked sessions with me. The night before I was to have my first appointment with Margarita, Brian's mother, I fretted—what could I possibly do or say that would help her deal with such an unfathomably painful loss?

"God, help me help her" was the prayer I chanted as I fell asleep.

Disappointingly, I awoke after no elaborate dreams. Only one thing stood out from the jumble of incoherent images I'd seen: the word *mosaic*.

As had become my practice over the past three decades, I dutifully wrote it in my dream journal. I'd become habituated not to evaluate but to take dictation and write my dream, like a dutiful secretary, even if the dream didn't make sense, even if it was ridiculous, and even if it seemed like it had nothing to do with my life.

Frustrated I had no clear image of what I wanted to say, I traced the word over and over on the page in my journal, so many times that *mosaic* left an indent on the next few pages. I couldn't help but look at this random word, *mosaic*, and think, *Really, God, that's the best you could do?*

I approached my session with Margarita carefully, tenderly, and with the intention of providing a space where she could feel safe enough to fully express herself. In our phone session, she shared feelings that ran the gamut from anger to devastation to shock to gratitude for the time she spent being Brian's mother. She talked about the more than eight hundred people who attended the funeral, most of whom referred to Brian as their best friend. Family and friends shared their favorite "Brian moment" and the special ways in which Brian had been a lighthouse in their life.

In the final moments of our session, as an afterthought, Margarita shared she'd received mountains of flowers and cards, but there was one special present she would treasure forever: a poster-size photo of Brian that one of those best friends had created. From afar, it looked like a single image of Brian smiling but viewed up close, the single picture was a mosaic, composed of hundreds of tiny Brian pictures.

Dumbstruck, I asked Margarita, "Did you say 'mosaic'?"

"Yes, this mosaic of Brian is so amazing. It shows what an incredible life Brian lived. I've been looking at it the whole time we've been talking."

I nearly fell off my chair. And when she texted me a photo of this masterpiece, it was time for my tears. I couldn't believe the incredible synchronicity.

After I told Margarita about my mosaic dream, we shared a stunned silence as a tremendous blessing began to reveal itself. We both interpreted this dream as a message from Brian letting her know he had survived death. And though he was no longer in physical form, he was intact, and the individual pieces of the Brian mosaic would live on, in the thoughts and memories of everyone who loved him.

Here's how we OGLE'd it:

O: *What is the Offending behavior and/or situation?*

Brian died. There's no greater offense than to be here one minute and gone the next, without warning, especially when someone was as amazing and intrinsic to life as Brian had been.

G: *What is Good about that offending behavior and/or situation?*

To our humanness, there's nothing good about dying. However, knowing we all have an expiration date gives us the ultimate opportunity to not take any moment we're alive for granted. What's good is not that Brian died but that he lived with so much joy, vigor, and generosity.

For me, this situation has made me feel even more convinced that life continues beyond the body. As for our dreams, if I wasn't already freakishly passionate about them, because of this I've become even more so—believing no matter how innocuous they may seem, they are worth a few moments of recognition.

L: *How am I peering into the Looking Glass (mirror)?*

Brian's family (of which I consider myself an honorary member) shared with me that his life, and untimely death, has inspired the entire community to be more Brian-like—to not just keep our gas tanks filled but to make sure to fill our loved ones' tanks with all

the love we've got. We never know when our last encounter with them will be.

E: *How will I allow this situation to Elevate me? What Elevated action will I take?*

Because of my connection to Brian via his family, I seem to meet people who confess how fun they think it is to test the limits of their empty gas tanks. I tell them the tale of Brian, followed with "Sorry to be a buzzkill, but for the love of God, don't play Russian roulette with your gas tank. When in doubt, fill it up!"

As icing on top of an already-decked-out cake, I have to mention that after my first session with Margarita, later that same day, my mother called to tell me about her and my dad's plan to move to the heart of vibrant Los Angeles from the sleepy suburbs. They had found a place to live. I'd been advocating for them not to move downtown. "City life is no place for retirees," I cautioned. I was worried about them and strongly suggested they consider a quiet place by the ocean, maybe even a retirement villa with other folks their age. I was upset they were acting like rebellious teenagers, lusting for a fast-paced, metropolitan lifestyle.

I was getting ready to make my case again when my mom told me the name of the apartment complex she'd fallen in love with. "It's called the Mosaic."

What?

In one second flat, I went from being thoroughly against their life-changing agenda to becoming their biggest cheerleader. It's been a few years since they moved in and out of the Mosaic. All I can say is their few years spent in the center of art and commerce gave my folks an exciting new lease on life. They're back in the 'burbs again, but they speak glowingly of their walk on the wild side, during which time they both lost weight, looked younger, and were the happiest they'd been in years.

I'm still in touch with Brian's family, and although they will always miss him tremendously, the mosaic dream became the first of many messages from Brian through dreams and "coincidences" to help them acclimate to life without his physical presence. Margarita said even though losing Brian broke her heart into a million tiny pieces, the Brian mosaic has become a sacred relic, a symbolic road map toward peace in her heart and mind.

After my first session with Brian's dad, Jay, he emailed me this note:

> One individual photo does not represent a person's life. But this mosaic of Brian gives the 360-degree view, as it's comprised of little individual moments that together make the whole. A mosaic is such a perfect symbol to represent my "B-man's" life, because in this one mosaic you can see how we are all part of a larger serendipitous work that includes moments and people instead of brushes and paint. This mosaic of Brian is special for us because Brian was the glue that bonded us, and so many communities of people, together—in such a joyous way. Also, he was not one to get caught in any of the small stuff; he had a knack for keeping the larger picture, the mosaic, in mind at all times.[31]

Claire-ity

Southern California

What comes out from dark times is a whole new person who has risen up and has crossed the bridge for a brighter world.

KIDADL.COM

When she entered my home office, it was as if the sun itself walked in. I was blinded by the inner and outer light of this petite fourteen-year-old girl. If Angelina Jolie and Anne Hathaway had a baby girl, she would've been Claire.

Her aunt, Blyss, my client, had been telling me for years, "You *have* to meet Claire. She's one of the most incredible humans on the planet. She has CF, cystic fibrosis, and spends most of her life in the hospital. Next time she's out, I'll bring her to you."

Then one day, Blyss chirped on the phone, "Today's the day. I'm gifting Claire my next session with you."

First, you must know, my front door is perched at the top of fifty steps. And my outdoor deck is another fifty steps beyond that. Had

I done any research ahead of time, I would've realized Claire would be lugging an oxygen tank behind her. I should've insisted on coming to her or meeting somewhere on level ground. Alas, Claire, led by Blyss, was not fazed by my steps. Sure, she was out of breath, as everyone is when they reach my porch, but she was buoyant as she exclaimed, "Wow, can I live here with you? This is my kind of treehouse!"

I loved her instantly and said a hearty, "Yes!" joking as I handed her the keys. "Take them; they're yours!"

I marveled at how, aside from the oxygen tank at her side and tubes running into her nose, she was a charming, vivacious, and surprisingly typical precocious teenage girl. However, I soon discovered the reason for Blyss insisting we meet.

As I made the three of us tea, I quickly learned, contrary to Claire's dazzling sparkle, how grueling her life was. Since infancy she had endured daily breathing treatments, followed by swallowing fistfuls of horrible-tasting medications and eating a high-calorie diet that would choke a sumo wrestler, all just to survive her condition.

Through her hilarious, self-deprecating sense of humor, Claire shared about how she was an expert in the art of hospital room decoration. On her long visits (sometimes months at a time), she'd bring rugs, lamps with decorative shades, fairy lights, essential oil diffusers, speakers to pipe in her music, not to mention her favorite blanket, pillows, and books to make her feel at home.

I asked her the story behind her peculiar email address: IVPoleRaces@blahblahblah.com. She responded with a wry smile, "I'm known for rousing the other kids, in the middle of the night, to race with me down the halls, using our IV poles like skateboards, when the nurses aren't looking."

After we finally settled into our session above the trees overlooking the canyon, Claire blew on her steaming mug of green tea as she shared her recurring dream with me. She said it started immediately following her revival from a coma she'd had only a 3 percent chance of surviving. She set her mug on the table, leaned in, and enchanted me with her inimitable raspy voice:

"In my dream, my best friend and I are walking through a playground, and we come across a twisted vine that catches our attention because it reminds us of 'Jack and the Beanstalk.' When we touch the vine, it carries us, at light speed, up to the 'galaxy.' High above the clouds, this is the most beautiful place I've ever seen. Up here, I don't need my oxygen tank or my medical treatments. I can run and do cartwheels, and I feel so free—like my best self, in every way. Not only is this place painted with the most brilliant colors, but it's also filled with the answers to our every question.

"For example, my best friend has boy problems, but in the galaxy, she completely understands why her boyfriend doesn't call or text when he says he will. Up here, it all makes perfect sense.

"I get the courage to ask a question I've always wanted to know the answer to: 'Why do I have this illness?'

"The answer is transmitted to me immediately through a sense of knowing: 'Your reward for being such a light to others in past lives is the gift, this time, of a short life. You won't have to grow old like so many other people have to. You will have a lot of friends, and because of your illness, you will connect with them in meaningful ways. In fact, your battle with cystic fibrosis will be a connecting link, allowing you to make a difference in the world by shining light on CF. You'll also share your message to the rest of the world about the preciousness of life . . . and then you'll get to leave, before you grow old.'

"With that, a phenomenal peace washes over me. This insight heals my heart because I'd always felt guilty, believing my illness was punishment for something I'd done wrong or because I was bad. But now I know that's not true.

"We continue to explore the galaxy for what seems like months—and then we remember our families back on earth. We panic because we don't want them to worry, so we slide back down the vine to earth as quickly as possible.

"Luckily, it turns out, in Earth time, we've only been gone a few minutes. What a relief.

"Then I receive a fancy invitation in the mailbox announcing I've been selected to be a Bridge Angel. I jump up and down in excitement like I won the lottery, even though I have no idea what a Bridge Angel is. But I discover, by on-the-job training, that a Bridge Angel escorts people who just died to the galaxy. Most people don't know how to get there on their own, so they need a Bridge Angel, like me, to take them. Since I know how to get there, and I totally love it, I'm perfect for this important job.

"Since then, for the past few months, every night, I'm at the bedside of a different person, who I don't know, at the moment of their death. They are confused, and at first they resist me, because they're so attached to their loved ones and their lives on earth. But once I tell them how amazing the galaxy is, I take their hand and say, 'Let me just give you a peek.' Once they see the galaxy, they smile so big, give me a hug, thank me, and move toward the light and their loved ones waiting to greet them.

"I have this dream a lot, nearly every night, and so far I've taken over a hundred people to the galaxy—all kinds, young, old, every ethnicity and religion . . . and they all die in different ways.

"It's so funny, because from the ordinary human perspective, death seems so tragic, but when I'm in Bridge Angel mode, it's magic—a door to another world, so much better than the one we live in here.

"But I learned the hard way, as a Bridge Angel, that I have to be very persuasive. Once there was a man so stubborn and attached to his earthly life that he wouldn't let me take him, so I gave up and let him go," she looked off in the distance, pensive. "I found out he became a lost soul. That's when I realized the seriousness of my job. Since then, no matter how much my clients resist me at first, I've never let them slip by."

When she asked what I thought her dreams meant, I was speechless—me, who never has a problem waxing poetic about even the most innocuous dream. When I finally found words, I simply said, "I think most dreams are symbolic—meant to be interpreted. But there are those special dreams that are a happening . . . a true event . . . a reality on a parallel plane. These dreams are to be reveled in and, perhaps, accepted as real. At the very least, when direct communication from the dream gods takes the time to spell out a message, like in this dream, it's to be treated like medicine. If it were my dream, I'd take it every day and let it strengthen and, perhaps, even heal me."

Though Claire wasn't religious, her "galaxy" certainly sounded like heaven to me. And Claire's Bridge Angel dream became a source of peace and reassurance for her and her family—especially her younger sister, Ellie. Because they shared a bedroom, Ellie would ask Claire to tell her Bridge Angel bedtime stories to help her sleep:

"Tell me again about the galaxy."

"What is it like to be a Bridge Angel?"

"When it's my time, will you be my Bridge Angel?"

"Do I have to wait till I die to visit you in the galaxy?"

Claire's stories would reassure Ellie and send her to dreamland with a smile on her face. With paints and pastels, Claire created pictures of the galaxy, so, like using a treasure map, Ellie would know where Claire would be when the time came.

Seven years later, despite all her daily breathing treatments, Claire's lungs progressively weakened, and on August 26, 2018, Claire and her family got word to rush her to UC San Diego hospital for a double-lung transplant. She'd been putting off this procedure until she no longer could. At first it seemed the surgery was a success, until days later, while she was recovering in the ICU, a blood clot cut off blood flow to the right side of her brain, resulting in a massive stroke.

In spite of the valiant efforts of the hospital staff and the thousands of friends and fans praying for her from around the world, on September 2, 2018, with a hospital waiting room packed with family and friends, Claire was escorted to the "galaxy" by her very own Bridge Angel.

Here's how I OGLE'd it:

O: *What is the Offending behavior and/or situation?*

Even though I learned from Claire that it can be a gift to leave this planet early, I couldn't help thinking from my conditioned human mind, of all people who should've lived to a ripe old age, it should've been Claire . . . no matter what they told her in the galaxy.

My spiritual self can find the beauty, but it's hard for my emotional and rational selves to make sense of why she had to suffer with this disease and why, with so many medical breakthroughs, there still isn't a cure for cystic fibrosis.

G: *What is Good about that offending behavior and/or situation?*

I imagine Claire would've lived an extraordinary life, CF or no CF. But because of her illness, she, and her mother and father, started the Claire's Place Foundation and have raised money for families who struggle with the disease.[32]

Her short life, lived with such concentrated inspiration, makes me look at the way I'm living—not wanting to waste my life or my breath on petty concerns, thinking I have the luxury of time . . . when none of us, myself included, know how long we have.

Besides me, Claire uplifted hundreds of thousands (if not millions) of people throughout her life through her TEDx talks and viral YouTube videos. In fact, she was the inspiration for the major motion picture *5 Feet Apart*, as well as a YouTube documentary about her, *Claire*.

I believe most dreams are a metaphor, but sometimes they are literal. In Claire's case, I believe she really was and probably still is a Bridge Angel who helps transport newly departed souls to the other side. Additionally, the message she received from her first foray into the galaxy about having the "gift of a short life" was a great blessing to me, personally—especially because of Tendral's early passing—and to all the others I know who've lost young loved ones.

L: *How am I peering into the Looking Glass (mirror)?*

If CF is the offending situation here, as the ultimate breath robber, I can link this back to myself by remembering when a shaman once told me to be mindful of how easily I breathe my power away (as I did in the past). He talked about how the addictive nature of human beings is to give power away to the highest bidder for attention. Each breath is an invitation to breathe back in the power I've unknowingly given away.

In the Looking Glass, I can also see my own inner Claire, who is the ultimate poster child for transforming the tragic into magic. With this book, I'm embracing my inner Claire by airing out my personal tragedies and crises (though seemingly small compared to hers), with the intent to inspire you. Inspiration, as it turns out, is related to inhaling. In the Looking Glass, I see Claire inspiring me to fill my lungs to the fullest capacity, so I may give my all before I expire with my last exhale.

E: *How will I allow this situation to Elevate me? What Elevated action will I take?*

One of the most inspirational things about Claire is she literally lived what is considered to be the most powerful way to live, as if death were over her shoulder.

If it weren't for Claire's CF, her message, and, dare I say, her mandate, she might not have become the role model she became as one who did not fear death.

Ancient dream cultures, like the Senoi of Malaysia, believe dreams are not only for the dreamer but are meant to be shared so the entire tribe might benefit. This is definitely the case for Claire's Bridge Angel dream.

My life has been elevated by spending time with the amazing Claire. I take comfort in knowing that when my time comes, I was among the first to put in dibs on her being my escort to the hereafter. Until then, I'll honor her by living a life I can be proud of, with the "Claire-ity" to not take a single breath for granted.

The Producer Who Wouldn't Sleep with Me

Southern California

"Congratulations," she said, "you booked the role on the TV series!"

"Oh my God!" I screamed into the phone. "I can't believe it." Adrenaline surged.

The smokey voice on the other end of the line was my agent, saying, "The president of one of the biggest entertainment companies in Hollywood, responsible for the most popular shows on television, likes your demo reel. You have a meeting with him, tomorrow. Make a good impression. Whatever you do, don't blow this."

After nine years of flailing in Tinsel Town, despite booking a few small parts in big productions (like *Leaving Las Vegas* and *ER*) and some big parts in small B movies (like *Death by Dialogue* and *Caged Fury*), I still had a negative bank account balance and was working for tips as a maître d' (glorified hostess) in a restaurant. Despite my attempts at an upbeat façade, behind the scenes, it was all I could do to stay one step ahead of depression, since my life had been filled with more rejection than a door-to-door refrigerator insurance salesman in the tundra.

My ever-resourceful, optimistic mother had given me a mason jar and a bag of one hundred pennies. She encouraged me to put a cent in the jar each time I got a no, and when I was done with all the pennies, the odds were I'd get a yes.

She was right. On this day, my pennies filled the jar, just in time for me to catch my lucky break. With this one phone call, I was drunk with relief and allowed the unrelenting pressure from the struggle of the last decade to finally cascade off my shoul-ders. *I can finally step away from the crowd of wannabes to the purified realm of working actresses.* I imagined I could now breathe champagne-scented air instead of sweat-infused desperation from casting cattle calls. No longer one of the herd, I'd been sin-gled out by the president himself. I felt like a plug who'd finally found her socket in the motherboard: zapped with energy, alive.

Despite my inability to eat or sleep, the next day I was completely alert, seated with my back ballerina-straight on a pristine, white, modern leather couch beneath a vaulted ceiling with skylights, gardenia air freshener subtly filling this shiny high-rise office. I was focused on breathing in and out, calming my nerves. I wore my "good luck" red-and-black gingham minidress with black high-heeled go-go boots. My nine-year-old self wanted to bust into a cartwheel, but luckily, I kept her under wraps.

I stood as Mr. President walked in with a confidence that filled the room. Early thirties, wavy light-brown hair—he wasn't movie-star handsome but still good-looking in his casual Armani business suit. Formal as he shook my hand, he gestured for me to sit. He looked me straight in the eye and said, "You're talented. But do you think you can handle the pressure of a weekly network series?"

I felt dizzy as a string of yesses uncontrollably sputtered out of my mouth: "Yes, yes, and yes!"

That night, I dimmed the lights of my North Hollywood apartment, wet hair in a turban towel, body wrapped in my plush, white bathrobe, clean from a long, hot bath scented with rose and lemongrass to calm me so I could sleep. As I turned off the stove to stop the kettle's whistle, signaling the hot water was ready to mix with my chamomile tea, the phone rang, sending alarm bells to quake my serenity. I glanced at the clock: nine.

Answering, I was shocked to hear Mr. President's voice on the other end of the line. Why would he be calling me after office hours?

"We're sending over your contract tomorrow. Your career is about to take off. You're about to start making real money."

"Oh my God." I wished I could stop saying that, but I couldn't. "Oh my God, I can't believe it."

"Well, believe it. But I have a question for you . . . what do I get out of this?"

"Huh?"

"What do I get out of this?" he repeated. "This role will change your life and put you on the map. I'm giving you every actress's greatest dream. So, what's in it for me?"

Feeling unsteady, I held on to the wall, like trying to keep steady during an earthquake. "Besides knowing you've picked the right girl for the part and me doing everything I can to make sure the show is a success?"

"No, honey. We're already successful. What's in it for me *pershonally*?"

I detected a slur. Was he drunk? My stomach dropped, and the darkness seeped in. "I'm not sure what you mean."

"Let me be direct. The only thing you have to offer in return for me changing your life is . . . sex. If we have sex, the part will be yours."

Silence, except for the pounding of my heart. My upper lip twitched as a hood of heat enveloped my head, making me woozy and disoriented. I felt like a cornered animal, knowing I couldn't run or hide, just turn over and expose my belly and admit defeat. But that didn't stop me from babbling, each syllable sounding more ridiculous than the last.

I spent the next thirty minutes trying every which way I could to convince him sex with me was a bad idea, that I was a much better friend than a lover. In the end, when he wouldn't budge, I compromised, so I could rationalize what he was proposing as if it were a date: "Well, at least take me out to dinner. . . . Then we can play it by ear . . ."

"No. I don't want to date you. I don't have time. I'm busy. Besides, I hate dating actresses; they're the worst. I just want to have sex with you. Either we have sex, and you get the part that will change your life, or we don't, and you go back to being a wannabe. Your choice. What's it going to be?"

He had to say the dirtiest word in my vocabulary, *wannabe.* I could feel myself falling into quicksand as I stammered, "I'll . . . c-c-call you back."

Smashed like a fly that had flown at full speed into a glass door—splat. My spirit couldn't have been higher, and now, here I was, flat out on my bedroom floor.

If this had been an isolated incident, I might have remained calm and clear. But because this was the domino stacked on top of a leaning tower of so many similar situations like this over the past decade, I felt overcome with despair.

To make matters worse, I was ripped in half. One part of me (the good, Catholic girl, with morals, from a good family) wanted to tell him to GO FUCK HIMSELF! OK, good Catholic girls would never tell someone to F off. But I at least wanted to say, "I would *never* do such a thing—how dare you!" Meanwhile, the other part of me, road weary from nearly a decade slogging through the entertainment industry, pleaded with me, *I've tried this business the honest way, and it hasn't worked! It's just sex. Who cares? Of all the men who've propositioned me, he's the best-looking—genuinely attractive-ish. His personality sucks, but he's young-ish and handsome-ish and not a complete troll . . . and this is an incredible offer.*

I lumbered to the bathroom and splashed cold water on my numb face to try to snap out of the trance. Just then I noticed the Shel Silverstein book with a dusty cover that had been sitting on the toilet-side table for months. I flipped to a random page and let my finger land on a line. I opened my eyes slowly, knowing this would be the Universe's guidance about what to do:

There is a voice inside of you

That whispers all day long,

"I feel that this is right for me,

I know that this is wrong."[33]

Damn. That was spot on. No interpretation required.

I felt dirty for even considering Mr. President's indecent proposal. I dialed him back and forced the words out of my mouth: "Thank you for considering me for this part. I am flattered by your offer. But as much as I want this role . . . I can't. If you change your mind . . ."

"You'll regret this," he barked, interrupting my soliloquy. The next sound I heard was the loud slam of his phone as it hung up, followed by the long, dull throb of the dial tone.

Goodbye, Mr. President, and goodbye Hollywood.

Suddenly lucid, I looked around and saw my path in Hollywood had been littered with men like him, luring me in at every turn. And what was my part in this ridiculous tango? I kept foolishly taking the bait.

To help me cope with my quarter-life crisis, an actress friend shared how hypnotherapy had helped her quit smoking by working with her subconscious—the part of the mind that runs the show of our lives. I remembered a therapist from years before telling me, "Dreams are the language of the subconscious."

I remembered being fascinated with dreams in my younger years, so I decided to try hypnotherapy. After a few months, healing began seeping in, and I enrolled in school to become a hypnotherapist myself.

A year later, I launched my business as a certified clinical hypno-therapist, a professional trained to help people break destructive habits and create more empowered lives. It turned out all the heartbreaks I'd lived through served to help me understand the terrain of other people's pain . . . which turns out to be a good trait for a therapist.

I felt proud of myself not just for no longer waiting tables and for no longer waiting for a casting director or Hollywood big shot to give me the green light to start living my life. Employing the empathy I'd developed as an actress (on the few parts I did get), I cultivated a thriving practice.

I began calling the shots in my life, leading workshops and writing what would one day be my first book. Then one day, through a satisfied client, I was given the opportunity to record high-quality hypnotherapy programs. With production expenses covered by my client, I was able to show up and do the work I loved to do in a way that, hopefully, would one day bring it to a larger audience.

Excitement mounted as I drove along the winding streets of Laurel Canyon, the imagination vortex where Joni Mitchell, Jim Morrison, and the Beatles once gravitated. The studio on Yucca Trail was nestled on a tree-lined cul-de-sac. Out in front, I spotted the producer my client wanted me to meet: a handsome man who reminded me of Richard Gere in *Autumn in New York*, with gray, slicked-back hair. The producer shook my hand and introduced himself as Dana.

I followed him past an ivy-covered gate into what looked like Frodo's hobbit home in *The Fellowship of the Ring*. As Dana guided me into his studio, I realized I was alone with him . . . in a remote space . . . and felt suddenly guarded.

My trauma from my casting couch near-miss kicked in. "Sorry if this sounds rude, but before we start, I have to know if you're going to pull the producer card and tell me that in order to work together, we'll have to sleep together," I said with my hand on my hip, point-blank.

Unruffled, he replied, "Don't flatter yourself."

That awkward moment was worth my discomfort. Having addressed this issue . . . it vanished. Without skipping a beat, he showed me to the vocal booth. Closing my eyes, I took a few deep breaths, envisioned working with a client, and launched in.

The recording session flowed, as did each subsequent session. Over the course of the next couple of years, Dana listened to me and encouraged my insights. I felt safe with him and seen.

At some point while working with him, I lost the self-doubt and trail of baggage I'd accumulated during my Hollywood days. Though I was supposedly "the healer," his respect was the healing.

Here's how I OGLE'd it:

O: *What is the Offending behavior and/or situation?*

What was so offensive were the many Hollywood types who lured me in, lied to me, and took advantage of my naïvety. They used their power to lord over me, making me feel small and helpless, feeding my weakness, insecurity, and desperation.

G: *What is Good about that offending behavior and/or situation?*

When I finally found Dana, I appreciated him for not being like the other producers. Without my past, I might not have valued his integrity as the resplendent treasure in the rough it was.

L: *How am I peering into the Looking Glass (mirror)?*

This one is difficult to write about. It's painful to admit that I've also abused my power and unconsciously learned from a young age the advantage of beauty's persuasion. The first time I heard the Eagles sing "Lying Eyes"—"City girls just seem to find out early how to open doors with just a smile"—I realized they'd written the song for me.

I never wanted to hurt anyone (because, frankly, I didn't consciously know what I was doing), yet I'm sure some of the same producers who misused their power on me were the same ones at whom I'd also batted an eyelash.

Ouch. Painful to admit. Ahhhh . . . the victim in me doesn't lay down her flag easily.

E: *How will I allow this situation to Elevate me? What Elevated action will I take?*

In the years following my foray in Hollywood, I paved my spiritual path brick by brick, one Elevated thought and action at a time. I worked hard every day to be mindful of my deep intent to use my life force for good, to empower, to support, to uplift, and to make the world (inner and outer) a better place.

Oh yes, I've learned my real mojo isn't skin deep—thank God, because physical beauty is a fleeting thing (and plastic surgery and Botox are expensive things). I learned about the notion of entelechy, a philosophical term brought to light by Aristotle, which refers to when the soul—a person's unique potential—is actualized in the body. Ahhh . . . my soul . . . that's where my true power resides, and no one can take that away—unless I give it to them.

A couple of years after meeting Dana and now so comfortable with him while we were working together, before we started recording, I complained about the guy I was dating. Midsentence, Dana raised his hand and said in his quintessentially direct tone, "I don't want to be your girlfriend."

Does that mean he wants to be my boyfriend?

This one statement flipped my world upside down and opened the floodgates of the feelings I'd been keeping at bay. It was such a strange thing to say—what could he possibly mean by that? I had to know. As I inquired deeper, what followed was our mutual confession about our love for each other . . . and how we both feared if we took our relationship outside the studio, we could ruin what we had. Ultimately, without coercion on either of our parts, we decided it was worth the risk.

Five years after meeting Dana at his canyon studio, in another canyon across town, amid squirrels, butterflies, friends, and relatives, we exchanged our vows in the backyard of our home.

It turned out the producer who didn't try to sleep with me became the one I did sleep with, and will sleep with, every night for the rest of my life.

I Never Let Go

Southern California

*One small crack does not mean that you are broken. It means
that you were put to the test and you didn't fall apart.*

LINDA POINDEXTER

A pack of men always made me nervous. Around them, my senses
heightened, flipping my fight/flight into high alert, as I heard
faint, whispered innuendos (sometimes not so faint) when I walked
through the fog of their cologne.

Packs reminded me of a time when I was a high school sopho-
more, at a sprawling backyard Hawaiian-themed party in Friendly
Hills, where the rich kids lived. All the pretty people dressed in
their best beachwear. I was like many of the other girls, clad in a
bikini halter top with a Hawaiian-print sarong with palm trees tied
around my waist, accented with a puka shell necklace I borrowed
from my mom's jewelry box to add a finishing touch. I remember
thinking I looked good that night. I was tan, wearing my signature

dayglow-pink lipstick, with my newly permed bushy, bushy blond hairdo, the likes of which I imagined inspired the Beach Boys to write "Surfin' USA."

My stomach dropped when I saw a senior from my school whom I not-so-affectionately called (in the privacy of my head) Jerk Face. He was hanging out with a group of good-looking, intimidating, college boys.

Why does he have to be here?

Jerk Face had a disapproving scowl and always seemed at the ready with a biting comment as we passed in the halls at school. Around him, I felt like I was on a stage facing a heckler with an arsenal of rotten tomatoes ready to be thrown in my direction at my slightest social infraction, or just for the heck of it.

Showing off in front of his college friends, he shouted, "Hey, Kelly, you think you're Miss Hawaiian Tropics, don't you?"

I rolled my eyes because I couldn't think of a clever comeback—I envied people skilled in the art of repartee. Jerk Face's jabs continued, and I shot back a lame but snarky, "You wish," with a dismissive flip of my wooly mane to compensate for my ineptitude at real banter. As ridiculous as my half-hearted comeback was, it must have cut him down because in a Greek chorus, the college guys groaned a collective, "OOOOOOOOH."

I turned my back and returned to sipping on my fruity piña colada, getting tipsy, chatting away with my friends, swaying to Izzy singing his "Somewhere over the Rainbow." As long as my back was turned toward the Neanderthals in Hawaiian shirts, I could block them out and have a good time. Or so I thought.

A half hour and another piña colada later, the party was in full swing. I don't remember exactly how it happened, but I was suddenly shocked to feel rough-as-sandpaper hands lifting me, carrying me as if on an invisible gurney, running me toward the dark, tree-lined outskirts of the property. Somewhere in the drunken swirl, I became aware my captors were Jerk Face and the college boys. The hand over my mouth muffled my scream. I kicked, but there must have been four or five of them. One guy at each of my arms, one at each leg, and one holding my mouth.

A surge of turbocharged adrenaline electrocuted me—no longer buzzed, I was suddenly hyper-awake, a cornered animal, fighting for my life. I wrenched my right arm free and grabbed a clump of hair from one of the guys, and I pulled it with Hulk-like strength.

"Let me go!" he shrieked like a girl in a horror movie.

I bit the hand on my mouth; when his hand retracted, I shouted, "I'll let you go when you let me go!" I pulled harder on the hair.

"Let her go!" he commanded his friends.

At once, they stopped, dropped my legs and loosened their grip enough for me to wiggle free. I shot like a rocket, a freed prisoner, running for my life toward the light of the house in the distance, bare feet scarcely touching wet grass. Dashing past sloshy partygoers in Hawaiian print, through the back gate, through the side door of the house, into the bathroom . . . Thank God, because of my tiny bladder, my superpower is a radar for knowing the most direct route to the loo.

I slammed the door, locking myself inside, crash-landing on the toilet. I sobbed at full voice, trying to catch my breath, looking down at my still-clenched, shaking right hand. I slowly peeled back my clamped-together fingers. To my horror, in my hand was a bloody clump of hair and skin . . . I never let go!

Holy shit! I scalped him!

I thought to flush it down the toilet but envisioned it clogging the plumbing, so I wrapped what looked like a murdered rodent in toilet paper and discarded it in the trash can.

As I washed my hands with scalding water and enough soap for my entire body, I watched my innocence, mixed with salty tears, mascara, and snot, whirl down the drain. I shuddered to think what would've happened had I not successfully grabbed that guy's hunk of hair. How would that night have ended?

Back at school, Jerk Face showed no remorse and didn't stop slinging biting remarks at me as we passed in the halls . . . which was a strange relief. I was all too eager to brush off what had happened and return to the status quo.

Here's how I OGLE'd it:

O: *What is the Offending behavior and/or situation?*

Drunken boys ganging up on a girl (me) is the offensive behavior—but Jerk Face was the real culprit in my eyes. He was my nemesis: on the lookout to pounce on me, to find fault. Because he saw me as a shallow bitch, I became one in his eyes. Being around him, even before that night, made my body and heart feel like a clenched fist—a recipe for bringing out my worst.

G: *What is Good about that offending behavior and/or situation?*

Before this situation, I never would've imagined I could have such strength—that I'd be able to access the ability to fight my way out of such an overpowering situation. I strangely feel like a badass just thinking of initiating a guy prematurely into membership in the Hair Club for Men. He's the one wearing a baseball cap when it's inappropriate to do so.

I give my sisters credit for helping me survive that night. It's because of our tussles growing up that I developed my biting and hair-grabbing expertise. Any girl who fights on a semi-regular basis knows that once you get ahold of someone's hair, the fight is over. Biting and hair-pulling might sound cute to a macho man, but I was one against five, and I got away (physically) unscathed.

L: *How am I peering into the Looking Glass (mirror)?*

Perhaps, in the same way I projected the villain on Jerk Face (and company), maybe that's how he saw me. Maybe I was so successful at masking my insecurities (like he must've done) that Jerk Face didn't see me quivering like a Chihuahua beneath my costume. He must've seen me as a "mean girl," someone to teach a lesson to, not someone to be kind to because she secretly wanted his approval. Maybe my scornful attitude, in front of guys he was trying to impress, was the ultimate emasculation. With one dismissive flip of my hair, I must've tossed his fragile ego beyond the tree-lined nether regions of the party, leaving him feeling cornered.

Note: In my willingness to peer into the looking glass in this situation, I'm not, at all, condoning Jerk Face's or his friends' deplorable behavior. Unkind words or scornful hair flips are never a rationale for rape (or near rape).

However, an empowered life comes from taking 100 percent responsibility for our energy and our actions. To alchemize the tragic into magic, the only behavior I have any say over in the matter is my own. And I'm willing to do the difficult job of seeing how my part might have contributed to this horrible situation.

E: *How will I allow this situation to Elevate me? What Elevated action will I take?*

It wasn't until many years later, in a late-night chat with my friends from high school, that I brought this story up, and they were shocked. I hadn't shared it with them before. I'd done what so many people do after an assault: bury the memory. *If I don't talk about it, maybe I can make it disappear.*

In writing this, I researched the topic and discovered that, according to *Psychology Today*, only one in five women who've been raped report it. The primary reason for this is, "From a psychological perceptive, these experiences can result in confusion and shock, often leading to PTSD. This type of trauma might be internalized as a coping mechanism and can take time to make sense of what has happened. But sometimes, triggering events cause these memories to resurface."[34]

What I know now that I wish I knew when I was sixteen is we're as sick as our secrets. Retroactively, I wish my past self would've talked about it with my mom or one of my closest friends . . . and maybe even reported it. Even though the situation didn't result in full-blown rape, what they did was not OK. The trauma of this experience burrowed inside me, and I unknowingly carried it with me, like a disembodied ghost, for decades.

At the very least, now, finally, I'm elevated in the awareness that I am more powerful than I realized—physically, emotionally, and spiritually. With power comes responsibility. I'm convinced that in most instances, the world is my mirror—when I'm in a bad mood and, without realizing it, treat people disrespectfully, I get it flung back to me, in spades. Alternatively, when I treat people with kindness and compassion, looking for the gold beneath their abhorrent behavior, they tend to treat me in a way that brings out my gold too.

I decided to imagine the apology Jerk Face would've given me, had he been in his right mind.

Jerk Face's higher self:

Kelly, I'm so sorry to have convinced my friends to gang up on you. You did not deserve that. My ego was so devastated by your dismissal of me in front of my friends, I reacted horribly. I wasn't seeing you as a whole person—just as someone I wanted to dominate to feel better about myself. I now see that way never works. Please forgive me. Also, I hope you'll see my taunting as a backward compliment—as a terribly escalated version of what boys do in grade school, where they pull the hair of the girl they like. I liked you and thought I didn't stand a chance . . . so I wanted you to hurt like I did. I'm glad you turned the tables on me and my friends: instead of us pulling your hair, you taught me/us a lesson by pulling out a clump of my friend's hair. Payback for our criminal-level stupidity. I'm so sorry. I hope in some way, in this life or a future life, I can make it right by you.

My elevated action is simply to forgive. I won't forget. Nor should I. But I no longer harbor hard feelings toward Jerk Face or his friends. I do pray, however, that whoever it was I scalped learned to hold women only with love, not with force.

Ding-Dong,
the Witch Is...

Southern California

I destroy my enemies when I make them my friends.

WIDELY ATTRIBUTED TO ABRAHAM LINCOLN

The morning after my apartment in the armpit of Hollywood got robbed, I was frantic to find another place to live . . . preferably one less armpit-ish. Even though I had nothing worth stealing, and my digs would never be featured on the cover of *Martha Stewart Living*, it had been my sanctuary. And the fact that the thieves ransacked my underwear drawer rattled me to my core.

I craved a haven from the storm that was my life. As I toured the rat-infested, ramshackle Hollywood apartments in my price range—which made my recently robbed apartment look like the Taj Mahal—my dreams were dashed.

Just when I was about to give up, I decided to look at one last apartment. It was way out of my budget. I'd been looking in the seven-hundred-dollars-a-month range, and this apartment was a whopping eleven hundred dollars a month, and it was in Beverly Hills, for God's sake.

There was a voice in my head shouting, *Are you crazy? You can't afford the luxury of even walking into a space that fancy.* But I was pulled by the other voice in my head, the angel, the devil, I couldn't tell which, when it tempted, *It doesn't hurt to look. What have you got to lose?*

Next thing I knew I was driving south along dazzling, palm-lined Doheny Drive. I approached the building carefully. The sunlight glinted a wink at me as I pulled in front and audibly gasped. I could swear the *Chariots of Fire* theme song was playing in the background as my body moved magnetically toward the gorgeous art deco building. It reminded me of the grown-up version of the dollhouse my grandpa built for my sisters and me. Light blue with bright-white trim, elegant, feminine, and whimsical.

I rang the doorbell and was greeted by the friendly building manager. With an inviting smile, he escorted me up the stairs to give me the tour of the vacant apartment. When he opened the door, I squealed in delight, as my entire body filled with sunshine. I felt like a princess who'd been living as a pauper and was finally reunited with her palace. OK, it was technically a studio where the living room and the bedroom were one and the same, but it was a palace to me. The way the hardwood floors reflected the natural sunlight made me feel so bright. I could never have a bad day if I lived here.

I didn't care if it was ridiculously out of my budget. I felt home for the first time since I'd left my childhood home in Whittier. I delighted in every gingerbread morsel of crown molding in the kitchen, the bathroom with its built-in vanity. I loved the way the afternoon glow filtered through the expansive windows.

I beamed as I vigorously shook my new landlord's hand without even considering if there were others in line for the place, so sure it was mine. "I'll take it."

A couple of weeks later I moved in and bought on credit a brand-new plush futon to be my bed by night and couch by day.

My new nest couldn't have been more magical and tranquil, except . . . occasionally, I was shocked by a pounding from below. My heart would stop, and my body would tense every time the angry woman with sensitive hearing downstairs pounded out her irritation when she heard my feet against the hardwood floor.

Within no time I learned to master the art of walking on air. I bought fluffy slippers I'd wear the moment I stepped into the apartment, so my high heels didn't so much as graze my floor. But even with my cloud-like feet flitting weightless like a ballerina's across the floor, her wrath would still get provoked, especially if, God forbid, I dropped something.

My hands shook when I transitioned my daytime couch into my nighttime bed, trying with all my Herculean might to ensure no wood-on-wood sounds could be detected. But when I fumbled, the broomstick from the trigger-happy witch downstairs was hell-bent on shattering my peace. After I received a nasty letter from her under my door calling me a rude lead foot and accusing me of stomping carelessly across my apartment, I furiously retaliated and slipped my reply under her door:

Dear Neighbor,

I'm sorry to be a pain in your ass. I don't mean to be. I, too, value my sanctuary, and you hitting the ceiling (my floor) with your broom handle is not my idea of home sweet home. You should know, I wear the world's fluffiest slippers. I'm working on levitating, but I still have a long way to go. I want nothing more than for you to have the peace you desire. I'm sure there's a solution. Until we find it, please back away from the broomstick.

Sincerely, your lead-foot, trying to be feet-of-feathers, upstairs neighbor,
Kelly

Months later, I was scheduled to audition for a go-go gig at a lesbian bar called the Icehouse in West Hollywood. To make enough to cover the rent for my fancy new apartment, I danced at the Palace on Fridays and Saturdays, the Mayan on Sundays, and Bordello on Tuesdays, taking Wednesdays and Thursdays to recover.

Around the back, I met the owner of the club, Phoebe, a heavy-set woman with a gravelly voice, baseball cap, and sleeveless Indigo Girls T-shirt. Once I was seated across from her in a cluttered office, she asked, "Are you gay?"

Before I could stammer my way out of saying no in a way that wouldn't blow my chances of getting the job, she jumped in, saying, "It's fine if you aren't, as long as you don't mind dancing for those who are. The lesbians here can be . . . a lively bunch."

"I don't mind at all. I can handle anything," I said, remembering all the grabby men I'd dealt with in the past. Men or women, straight or gay, the work was all the same. Or so I thought.

"Let's see how you do tonight. And if we all still like each other at the end of the shift, we can discuss you coming back next Monday. Come, let me take you to your cage . . ."

Cage? What kind of gig was this?

After I removed my pedestrian clothes and was left in my standard short-shorts, bustier, and cowboy boots, I followed Phoebe's stocky frame through the raucous club filled with various shades of lipstick lesbians, biker chicks, butches, femmes, tomboys, and jocks gyrating on the dance floor.

We arrived at the cage: a six-foot-by-six-foot cube that was not stationary, as I'd imagined it would be. It was hanging by a gigantic hook seven feet in the air. Phoebe rolled over a ladder to help me climb in, and I wanted to yell, "Are you insane?" But my inner Barbie doll persona took over; I swallowed my feelings and plastered on a fake smile as I climbed into a birdcage built for one. I imagined Maya Angelou reciting her famous poem "I Know Why the Caged Bird Sings" just for me, in rhythm with the four-on-the-floor house beat.

Shaky, I tried to get used to the swaying of my birdcage and its responsiveness to my every move. Phoebe gave me a thumbs-up and walked away. Like a baby bird learning to fly, I started with small dance moves, barely swaying side to side, grateful for the strobe lights casting shadows, a perfect device to distract club-goers from getting a good eyeful of my awkwardness.

Eventually I gained a little confidence, and while holding steady to the bars, I began whipping my hair around to the music. A hip-hop girl at heart, I wasn't a fan of rave music with a Euro-techno beat droning on at a spastic tempo, but I made the most of it. My job as ambiance in a bustier afforded me the ability to do some serious people watching while I gained enough balance to hurl myself around like a thundercloud in my midair prison. I was getting paid to have a tantrum in rhythm with the fast-paced music. And my mind was a calculator, trying to solve the case of my dwindling bank account. How could it be I was dancing my butt off (literally) yet still losing money? Without skipping a beat, I realized I was spending more than I was bringing in. No wonder I was broke. Then it became clear: my beautiful apartment was the culprit. I loved it—except for the witch downstairs. Was I going to have to find a cheaper place to live?

Thrashing around in my cell, imagining having to forgo my grown-up dollhouse—my refuge from the storm—shot dread through my veins. But as hard as I tried to fight it, I couldn't stop equating my self-worth with my net worth, all while I held my breath when I withdrew money from the ATM. I feared that instead of twenty-dollar bills coming out, a wrinkled, reprimanding hand would emerge and slap me. Dancing was my therapy as I attempted to exorcise my demons, unconsciously believing the pain I inflicted on myself made me like the thirteenth-century Roman Catholic flagellants, who paid penance to earn their way back into God's good graces. But on this night, it didn't work. Depression slid in anyway and slipped a dark hood over my head. Even in hyper motion, I couldn't outrun my inner witch. She caught me. As I surrendered, mid-hair-flip, it hit me: I tiptoe around my thoughts the same way I tiptoe across my apartment, trying to not trigger the witch. As awful as my downstairs neighbor is, she's a pussycat compared to the witch within.

I forced my body to keep moving to the cartoonishly fast beat, since the number one rule of go-go dancing is "don't stop moving," thus the name. I continued to unspool the unraveling thread. With the witch downstairs, no matter how hard I tried, she found reason to pound her broomstick. With my inner witch, even though I had a respectable (relatively speaking) dancing job, she still berated me for not making enough money. Sandwiched between both witches, there was no winning.

But even here, even though I was dancing as fast as I could, the witch was still able to seep inside the cage and catch me. In my first-ever remembered dream, when I was five, I dreamed of being chased by a witch, running, hiding to avoid her wrath. As I danced, desperate to escape her, I threw my head back, trying to pierce beyond the roof of my cell, and sent out a silent prayer for help: *God. I need a miracle. This witch has been chasing me my whole life. Help me find a way out of this inner and outer prison, now!*

Just then, an aggressive tribe of women with combat boots and flannel shirts startled me back to the present, howling at me like a pack of wolves. One started jumping, trying to grab my cage bars, desperate to reach in and touch me. Luckily my cage was above her head. I may not have been beyond reproach, but I was grateful to be beyond her reach. Not deterred, cheered on by her tipsy friends, she stepped back to get a running jump and missed. But on her next try, she sprang high enough to grab my cage bars and hoisted herself, with help from her inebriated tribe. Shocked, I smashed my body flush along the back of the cage as she shook the bars on the front, reaching her hands through, looking wildly into my eyes. Then with shock, she became suddenly sober and exclaimed, "Hey, I know you!"

I had no idea who she was, although there a vague familiarity about her.

"You're my upstairs neighbor. I'm Charlene; my friends call me Charlie," she shouted, gobsmacked, hanging on to the outside of my jail cell. "You're the one who makes all the noise."

What? Holy God. No way. Could it be? I'd never gotten a good look at her before. But I recalled her square-jawed profile from a passing moment by the lobby mailboxes. I had no idea she was the angry person who lived beneath me. I'd pictured a weathered old crone. But lo and behold, it was the witch downstairs herself, in the flesh, sans broomstick—younger and butchier than I'd imagined. The witch downstairs now had a name: Charlie, queen of the West Hollywood lesbians, and she was trying to break into my cage.

Charlie jumped down and pointed at me as she shouted to her friends, "She's the one I've been complaining about, the lead foot who lives above me—who makes my life miserable!"

They looked up at me and fell over themselves, cackling, giving her high fives and fist bumps as their dancing escalated into a frenzy, encircling my cage, beaming at me through disco lights, waving arms in rhythm with the spastic music. I imagined they were cavewomen around a fire, and I was their captured prey—and they didn't know whether to worship or eat me.

I was flooded with disbelief and relief that my nemesis, unmasked, was now a rosy-cheeked, warm-blooded human being. Charlie and I couldn't stop shaking our heads at the hilarity of it all, laughing about the bizarreness of our meeting. Somehow, because we met in my place of employment and her place of enjoyment, we now had an understanding about each other, bringing us to a miraculous truce.

That night, while unlocking the door to my lovely apartment, I juggled my purse and duffel bag and accidently dropped my keys to the floor. My breath caught in my chest as my entire body clenched. It was three in the morning. I cringed, waiting for the broomstick to begin its disapproving pounding. But to my surprise and relief, all I heard was delicious silence. In fact, from then on, even when I walked too loudly across the floor or dropped my futon to the ground with a thud, I never heard another angry sound from her or her broomstick.

Here's how I OGLE'd it:

O: *What is the Offending behavior and/or situation?*

The way the witch downstairs pounded her broomstick at my every misstep, wrecking the peace for which I was paying a high price in this expensive apartment. She was hypercritical of me, demanding the impossible and causing me to live in a constant state of tension and fear.

G: *What is Good about that offending behavior and/or situation?*

She had the self-esteem to demand what she needed and felt she was entitled to: peace and quiet. Her sensitivity, like anyone's, is where our greatest gift resides as well as where we're tortured, until we discover a solution.

L: *How am I peering into the Looking Glass (mirror)?*

We both wanted the same thing: a serene place to live.

I also realized I was more critical of myself than she could've ever been . . . pounding my own (invisible) broomstick at my every real or perceived infraction.

If I look more deeply at my inner critic, I can also see she just wants a better life for me, even if her communication style sucks and is questionable and quasi-abusive.

E: *How will I allow this situation to Elevate me? What Elevated action will I take?*

Joseph Campbell describes the meeting with the goddess on our hero's journey: "The ultimate adventure, when all the barriers and ogres have been overcome, is commonly represented as a mystical marriage . . . of the triumphant hero-soul with the Queen Goddess of the World."[35] The former witch downstairs handed me the mysterious key I'd been praying for, to release me from my own confinement. Next time I find myself judging someone without taking the time to get to know them, I'll pound my own broomstick on my floor to get my attention and wake me up to remembering people are not always what they seem. In fact, the enemy is often a rosy-cheeked ally in disguise.

Splat

Arizona

> *Jump off the cliff and learn how to make*
> *wings on the way down.*
>
> RAY BRADBURY

I don't know whose brilliant idea it was that inspired me and my dear friend Anastasia to put our lives in peril. It must've been the tan, tequila-touting, chiseled hottie who let us sunbathe on his boat.

All I did know was that it was spring break, and I desperately needed to cut loose. I'd been working hard making poor decisions in my so-called acting/singing career, and when Anastasia suggested a trip, the call of the wild reached in and grabbed my soul.

Anastasia pouted, "Come on! It's only a few days . . . a long weekend . . . what could it hurt?"

My worlds clashed, and I felt torn like a cheap rope in a tug-of-war against two muscled opponents. It unhinged me to be on the receiving end of my then talent manager's disapproval and, worse, losing his respect for taking frivolous time for R and R. But I also felt I couldn't let Anastasia down.

I told her I'd sleep on it. All night long I dreamed of gorgeous guys and girls in the prime of their lives, frolicking in the lake, while I sat alone, staring like a voyeur through a thick plate-glass window. I sprang out of bed the next morning, called Anastasia, and told her to get her bikini ready and make us some PB and Js for the road.

Eight hours later we arrived in scorching Lake Havasu on the Nevada/California/Arizona border just in time to pull into a nearby nightclub, and we danced and laughed the night away. For a snapshot in time, I felt like my old self—a fun party girl, cutting loose, without a care in the world about my damn career.

The next morning resembled my dream and a quintessential spring break movie. Anastasia and I were surrounded by girls in candy-colored string bikinis, flirting with shirtless, muscled guys on a blistering afternoon while thrumming music ricocheted across the lake. We lounged on the yacht belonging to the cute guys we'd danced with the night before, drinking in the nectar, letting my thirsty soul be quenched as we sang along with Cyndi Lauper's "Girls Just Wanna Have Fun."

In the center of the yahooing reverberating through the canyon, our eyes met up with the main event: our drunk peers taking turns jumping off a sixty-foot cliff into the water.

Next thing I knew, a boatful of our new friends rallied us to join them in becoming part of the spectacle. Against the loud no in my belly, my inner thrill-seeker got whipped up in the frenzy and followed Anastasia and the others, barefoot, up the side of the cliff.

What I didn't realize when I was gawking from the safety of the boat below was how treacherous this was. Every step up this jagged incline was a struggle as my feet nearly slipped with each shaky advance up the shifting rocks. Looking down, I had the horrifying realization that the farther I climbed, the more perilous it would be to change my mind and recede. There would be no backtracking. I had no choice but make it to the top and jump.

My adrenaline fired rockets as we approached the summit. Anastasia stood ahead of me on the ledge with room enough for only one person. On deck, I was crouched below her, impatiently awaiting her splash letting me know it would be my turn to get this nightmare over with. But the sound didn't happen. I looked up to see Anastasia's fright manifested in her becoming a human ice sculpture.

I dared to peer over the edge of the cliff to see hundreds of people on boats waaaaaaay below, looking like chia seeds from up here. The sound echoed as they chanted, "Take it off," insinuating that not only should my frozen friend jump into the water sixty feet below but she should have the presence of mind to flash her boobs for their entertainment as she leaped.

I whispered, "Don't listen to them. And you'll be OK. Just take a deep breath, and when you're ready, jump. I'll be right behind you."

As much as my pep talk was for Anastasia, it was also for me because I couldn't jump until she did, and every second we spent there caused my horror-o-meter to rise. I, too, was in jeopardy of freezing if I didn't jump soon. To make matters worse, there was a growing line of impatient people now crouched behind me.

I fought to hold on to a frayed shred of lucidity, barking orders to myself: *When you hear Anastasia's splash, slowly count to five to give her time to swim out of the way and then throw yourself into the water.*

Then I finally heard Anastasia's scream followed by a splash. With my heart pounding out of my body, I counted to five, propelled myself into a standing position, and without taking a moment to collect myself, squeezed my eyes to block out the circus below . . . and with all my determination, I flung myself off the cliff.

My body twisted and scrambled in midair, legs thrust out in front of me, until I heard SMACK as I hit the water, followed by numbness.

When I finally bobbed up, the crowd cheered . . . because I was alive. Instead of landing the way a person should, tiptoes first, with arms crossed in front of their chest, I landed with legs jutted out in front of me, parallel to the water.

If I'd landed flat on my back, my injuries could've been much worse, even fatal. But instead, by a slight twist of fate and wind, I landed on my ass—the one I'd always complained was too meaty. I imagined the TV news announcer reading:

"Fat ass saves girl's life. News at eleven."

Once hoisted onto the boat, I began to feel the searing pain. My entire back and rear end turned from Coppertone tan to midnight blue. I was a walking bruise . . . but at least I was walking, by the grace of God. Even though I was in pain, I was grateful to *feel*.

Here's how I OGLE'd it:

O: *What is the Offending behavior and/or situation?*

Allowing myself to get swept up in the quasi-peer-pressure that led me to think it was a great idea to jump off a cliff, while tipsy, nearly killing myself or breaking my back.

G: *What is Good about that offending behavior and/or situation?*

I hope my cautionary tale (kids, don't try this at home) will prevent you or someone you know from participating in the same antics I did. If so, I won't feel like my foolishness was in vain.

L: *How am I peering into the Looking Glass (mirror)?*

I'm ashamed to say that I, too, have been the peer pressure-er. In the early days of my relationship with my husband, we were enjoying a lovely, relaxing visit in our friend's backyard. Next thing I knew, I was flying across their backyard on their newly installed zip line. I screamed to the heavens in pure delight with Jane of the Jungle exhilaration. I exclaimed, "Hubby! You have to try this."

He looked up at me from the comfort of his Adirondack chair, took a sip of his iced tea, and simply said, "Nope."

I pouted, stamping my foot. "Come on! It's so much fun. You'll love it. Please, do it just for me."

"Nope. You go ahead; it's not my thing. I don't have a good feeling about it," he responded, holding his ground.

But, like bratty Veruca Salt from *Charlie and the Chocolate Factory*, I demanded that he share in the joy I was experiencing. So, I did something I will regret for the rest of my life. It was not my finest moment, to say the least. I wish I could say I was abducted by aliens or a demon possessed my body, but I uttered the worst thing a wife can say to a husband: "Don't be a pussy."

To that, Dana said, "Fine." He had no choice but to set down his drink, rise from his comfortable chair, and climb the ladder. He strapped himself to the zip line, and when he was halfway across the yard, the line snapped. Dana fell to the ground in a nightmarish heap, dislocating his shoulder and knee.

It took nearly an hour for the ambulance to arrive, during which time Dana writhed in pain. We spent hours that night in the hospital, with me sobbing, pelting him with a nonstop torrent of apologies. "I am so sorry . . . I'm so, so, soooo sorry. I will never, ever do that again. I get it: no means no. Thank you for taking one for the team to teach me this valuable lesson to never push any-one into doing anything they don't want to do. How dare I claim to know what's better for any other living soul? I'm such an ass. Please forgive me."

E: *How will I allow this situation to Elevate me? What Elevated action will I take?*

I'd like to say that ever since that day, I've stopped encouraging peo-ple to take risks, but I'd be lying. I am, however, more attuned, like never before, to notice when somebody gives me a definitive no, and I remember when Dana (and I) went *SPLAT.*

In these moments, I stop, take a breath, and refrain from being a know-it-all. I'd also like to say I'm no longer a leap-before-I-look kind of gal, but again, I'd be lying. However, these days I am more prone to say, "Let me dream on it" before making a decision that might put my life or someone else's in harm's way. I now know I'm 100 percent responsible for what I do. People can cajole all they want, but in the end, my actions and their consequences are mine.

Speaking of consequences, I heard through the grapevine peo-ple are no longer allowed to jump off the cliff at Copper Canyon. I wasn't the only one who landed poorly. I'm sad to report several people severely hurt themselves, and a few even died.

Taking a risk is gutsy, sometimes foolish, sometimes smart, and sometimes what we do when we have no choice. Either way, taking a leap of faith beyond the security of our comfort zone comes with no guarantees; otherwise, it wouldn't be a risk—it would just be a step or a move.

I don't think I'll ever give up my ready-aim-fire MO, but like with anything, I want to have it without it having me. Sometimes the only way to make a quantum leap toward a new life or an up-leveled point of view is to take a risk.

Perhaps we ought to treat alchemy, ogling our tragedies, like it's our job. That way even if we leap and fall on our asses, once we put ourselves back together—even if we don't discover our wings, in this life or the next—we'll at least have learned (and earned) a little wisdom.

Pole Dancing in the Pandemic

Southern California

You may not control all the events that happen to you,
but you can decide not to be reduced by them.

MAYA ANGELOU

After watching the Netflix documentary *Stripped Down, Rise Up* through a stream of tears, I was, once again, reminded of my experience in my early twenties when I used to be a pole dancer—but not in the empowering way the film's Sheila Kelley encourages for women at her S-Factor studios.

On a Saturday afternoon just before the lockdown due to the COVID outbreak, my next-door neighbor Fox arrived, breathless on my front porch. "Kelly, I have to show you the new stilettos that just arrived in the mail for my pole-dancing class."

I gently shushed my new-to-America Siberian friend, innocent, talking taboo at full voice in front of my cedar-and-sage-wooded Topanga home. "Shhhhh . . . you don't want the neighbors to hear you." I whisper-shouted as I whisked this tall, graceful beauty through my front door before she could echo any more incriminating utterances through the canyon.

Like a wide-eyed child at Christmas, she plunked her lanky body on my faux-sheepskin-covered ottoman and tore the Amazon packaging. Squealing, she slipped on the most gargantuan pair of gold platform heals I'd ever seen, like chandeliers for feet.

"Kelly, you have to come with me to my pole class. It's exercise, but you get to wear high heels, like these, and act like a sexy stripper," she effused while modeling her shoes, her head nearly hitting the ceiling fan. "You can be my guest. You'll love it."

I tasted bile in the back of my tightening throat, stopped breathing, and tried to hide my heated face, as my Pandora's box fell off the shelf, releasing a circus of memories I'd stuffed away after that reporter (I mentioned in the introduction of this book) had nearly scandalized me a few years back. Even though I'd started an outline for what might be my tell-all book, I hadn't yet taken the plunge into writing, let alone publishing, my story . . . and was shocked at how electrocuted I felt. I tried to keep my cool as I replied through gritted teeth, "Wow, it's a workout, huh? Who knew?"

Oh, I knew . . . all too well. Though unable to move my mouth to form words, in my head I scolded Fox in a melodramatic huff. Why, in God's name, would I want to do something for pretend I used to do for real? Why would I want to do something as a workout I've been trying to work out of my system for the past thirty years? Why would I want to do something as exercise that I've desperately tried to exorcise from my psyche? And why would I want to do something that the very thought of brings up layers upon layers of insults, like a Russian doll—pun intended—triggering painful memories of sour bar fruit, beer-fueled, grabby hands, ruinous scandal from a chapter of my life I've had to tuck away into my innermost cave, so no scrap of gold sequin, silver lamé, or loose boa feathers could ever be detected by anyone?

I remained mute while exploding on the inside. Fox cocked her head, squinted. "Kelly, are you all right?"

I made an excuse about not feeling well. I shooed her and her monstrous shoes out of my house, but I couldn't rid the feeling of shame left in her absence. Then I flashed on my straight-talking New York writing mentor, Sue Shapiro, who parlayed the wise words of her shrink who'd said, "To stay clean, sober and healthy, you should lead the least secretive life you can."[36]

In the months that followed, thanks to the cave time afforded by the shelter-in-place mandate, I had an excuse for rebuffing Fox and her invitations, and I tackled the process of finally writing my story, secret by secret, humiliation by humiliation. As I came clean to myself about my past—which would be tame to some people, wild to others, and big to me—I felt genuinely relieved and surprised I hadn't been struck by lightning, the world hadn't stopped spinning, nor had a single limb fallen off my body.

Six months into quarantine writing, I ran into a masked Fox by our community mailbox. She shared, now in a hushed voice, that due to the pandemic, her pole dance studio was closed. So, she had installed her very own pole in her house. "You have to come see it and dance with me . . . you'll *love* it."

A week later, feeling nervous and ridiculous, with a mask slapped across my face, I forced myself to show up at her front door.

Fox answered the door with smiling eyes and a hot-pink, glittery face covering. Beckoning me inside, she introduced me to her shiny pole. In her Russian accent, she attempted her best Tony Montana from *Scarface*: "Say hello to my little friend."

Laughing, grateful for the icebreaker, I took a deep breath. Then, spellbound, I took in the pole's luster for the first time in thirty years, and it stirred within me a whirlwind of anxiety.

Six feet apart, with the pole between us, Fox led us through a brief warm-up. As we stretched, I was grateful to be surrounded by soft music, dim lights, glowing candles, and sweet, musky incense. This womb-like atmosphere was a radical departure from the environment I'd associated with pole dancing: blaring music, bright strobe lights, greedy hands. And instead of wearing a lacy G-string, high heels, and a push-up bra, on this day I was barefoot, wearing cotton leggings and a tank top.

As I sat midstretch, legs splayed in a quasi-split, a little voice screamed in me to take the risk and confess my secret to her. But I was torn because I was terrified of being judged, especially by someone I see frequently. Before I could rationalize a hundred reasons not to, I blurted, "Fox . . . I used to do this . . . for real . . . years ago . . . and being here is bringing up . . . memories . . ."

Her eyes widened as she gushed, "Wow, that's so cool."

I cocked my head. "Cool? Thank you, but that's the last thing I thought you'd say."

"My friends and I from the pole studio think strippers are rock stars! We all wish we had the guts to do it, even just for one night. What was it like?" she asked with wonder—like I'd just returned from a moon landing.

Though I was involuntarily shaking, I decided to trust her. With a quivering voice, I recounted what had happened thirty years before, when my twenty-one-year-old self, an ambitious baby bird, flew from the nurturing nest of my childhood home in the 'burbs into the wild windstorm of Hollywood.

I was broke, struggling to make it on my own, too proud to move back home when a producer with his name on gold records and movie posters strewn about his studio promised he'd make me a star. With his words, a hungry animal awoke in me. Besides, I didn't feel inspired or qualified to do anything else. I was a lousy waitress, and I hated accounting, so becoming a star felt like my only career option—a sink-or-swim situation.

A few months later, a sucker for his vision of my success, I fell for his suggestion that while he was shaping my career on "the fame fast track," I should dance at a gentleman's club to earn easy money. "You'd be dancing in a bikini—not naked—in front of an audience, so by the time your record deal is in place, you'll have zero stage fright. It's what Madonna did before she became a star. If you do this, I'll have more respect for you," he went on, "because it will prove you have what it takes."

I thrashed around internally, not because there was anything inherently wrong with stripping but because my identity was hell-bent on being a good Catholic girl, proving to all the kids from school that they were wrong about me. But in the end, my manager won out. I promised myself it would just be for a night, then a week, then two weeks, then three. . . . It wasn't until eighteen months later that I finally threw my pink duffel bag full of negligees in the trash. Despite my love affair with the pole itself, my shimmering stairway to heaven, my sanctuary amid the dank sleaziness of those clubs, that time in my life remained my shameful secret . . . and even led me to contemplate the pros and cons of the various ways I could end my life.

After I ditched the pole thirty years before, I worked diligently to regain a place of respectability in my inner and outer worlds.

Thanks to the blessing of skilled therapists, arduous recovery meetings, stacks of self-reflection scribbled in tear-stained diaries, and earth angels in cahoots, I pulled myself out of the Hollywood underworld, toward a life that today I love.

"The only problem is," I concluded, "all my decades of therapy and this past year I've spent writing righted much of my shadowy thoughts and feelings. But I don't think my healing can be complete until I bring my physical self into the mix."

Fox blinked away tears and touched her heart. Giving me a giant air hug, she said, "Kelly, thank you so much for sharing this with me. You're so brave. I'm honored you confided in me." She took a deep breath and asked, "Are you open to having a new experience of dancing with the pole?"

I nodded, feeling lighter. She stood and slowly pirouetted around the room. "All the space in this room is the feminine element. It's vast, mysterious, flowing." Grabbing ahold of the pole, she said, "The pole is the masculine element—sturdy, reliable, here to hold you as you lean on, push against, and swing around him. He is quite noble, despite all that gets projected on him. He just wants to be your sturdy hero, to help you find your wings."

She invited me to come closer to it, flirt with it, walk around it to the beat of the music—all the while barely touching it. I closed my eyes and invited in my prodigal self from the shadow lands. As my hips began to sway, I greeted my steely ally, in a thirty-year overdue integration celebration.

If it weren't for COVID, I would've given Fox the biggest hug for providing me with this glorious new reframe. When I left her home, I walked taller than before I entered, without need for stilettos.

On my second session, Fox rented her pole studio for us. After she led us through a few warm-up stretches, I approached the pole again, more boldly this time. Taking a deep breath, I shrieked with delight, surprised when I was able to spin and defy gravity like I'd done three decades before. It didn't matter I wasn't as graceful or nimble as I was back then—the fact that I was still able to feel the magic of liftoff was a miracle. I even surprised myself by remembering a few of my old moves from back in the day.

On our third session, I brought a playlist of music I loved. I felt lighter, less emotionally charged, and even more excited to reunite with my old friend (the pole) and see what healing magic we could create together. I bounded in, almost without saying hello. Fox had to hold me back, cautioning me to stretch before going too wild, to prevent injury. She taught me a few new moves I was ecstatically able to replicate, and I left feeling sore but elated.

On our fourth session, the mask felt stifling, and my joints were stiff. I was disappointed I wasn't able to pull off the same level of movement as I had the session before—or so I thought. Fox filmed me on my phone, so I could see my progress, in spite of how clunky I felt. Upon watching the video replay, I realized feelings aren't facts. I was shocked to see I was more graceful than I felt . . . good enough to give me the motivation to show up for our next session and the next and the next.

Here's how I OGLE'd it:

O: *What is the Offending behavior and/or situation?*

The big offender in this situation was my old manager from three decades before, who preyed on my innocence and gullibility. He manipulated me into stripping off not only my clothes but my self-respect as well.

At first, I was offended by Fox for being so free with her body and her choices, for having no shame in her game and relentlessly reminding me of the past I didn't want to face.

G: *What is Good about that offending behavior and/or situation?*

What's good about my old manager—besides that he's now six feet under—is he was the Hades to my Persephone. He lured me into the underworld, which nearly killed me but didn't. Because my twenty-one-year-old-self ventured into the dark, nearly died, and found her way back, not unscathed but intact, who I am today is wiser and more compassionate than I would otherwise be. Because I stripped off my dignity during my tour de force in the underworld, I can relate to people's heartbreak and bring them toward the light, because I know the way. And soon I'll have a book out about the whole ordeal, entitled *Stripped: Dancing with My Demons in the City of Angels*. I pray it will serve as a cautionary tale to other young women, and hope to help older women who have yet to come to peace with their reckless pasts.

I'm also grateful for Fox reconnecting me with the pole. It turns out healing can't be a 360-degree experience until the physical plane is included. Besides, I ended up having a lot of fun I didn't realize I was still capable of having.

L: *How am I peering into the Looking Glass (mirror)?*

Perhaps my soul self (certainly not my conscious-level ego) must have known I needed these experiences to become who I am today. No one ever held a gun to my head. It was me who took my first and last twirl around the pole. Maybe it was me who orchestrated the whole thing, and maybe it was me who put myself in front of Fox so I could eventually heal (and not the stiletto kind).

E: *How will I allow this situation to Elevate me? What Elevated action will I take?*

Now that I have swung full circle, like the women in the *Strip Down, Rise Up* documentary, embracing my inner pole dancer means I've reclaimed my body, the one that's been in perimenopause for the past couple of years. With each twirl around the pole, I build muscle, lose inches, and heal the shame I used to carry.

There's no denying how absolutely horrible the COVID-19 outbreak was—with so many deaths, other losses, and economic hardships. However, I believe, as the title of this book suggests, that a crisis is a terrible thing to waste. If we go through something difficult, we owe it to ourselves to look for and find the blessings in disguise. In that spirit, being homebound gave me the time and space to recover the sarcophagus of my twenty-one-year-old, G-string-wearing, lacy-bra-wearing, pole-dancing self. I learned to love her back to life—not so she might return to the beer-soaked catwalk from whence she came, but to celebrate her chutzpa, bravery, and fortitude.

These days, when I see a serviceperson climbing a telephone pole, hear tales of children skipping around a maypole, or am introduced in a virtual meeting to someone from Poland (ha ha), instead of burying my head, I smile because pole dancing has transformed from being a source of shame into an activity that supports the recovering of my sensual, feminine self—and for that, I'm grateful to open my wallet and pay for the experience. How ironic.

Cosmic Lola

Southern California

> *Act well your part; there all the honor lies.*
> ALEXANDER POPE

"And Lola removed her dog suit," I exclaimed in my dream, in the middle of the night, just hours before her Chiweenie body (half-Chihuahua, half-dachshund) would make her transition from earth to heaven. Lola unzipped her dog suit, like it was a child's onesie, and revealed the cosmos . . . and I was awestruck.

I met Lola eighteen years before, when the new landlord of my stepdaughter, Meesha, decreed, "No dogs allowed." Meesha was at a loss—her mother would've taken her, but she lived out of state, and no one else stepped up. I hate to admit I understood why.

Even though most people would consider me a "dog person," I really wasn't. Certain dogs touched my heart . . . and others, well, didn't. With her, let's just say, it wasn't love at first bite. She ran around my house, nipping at my heels, barking in an earsplitting

"YIPE!" followed by an entitled look on her stern face, reprimanding me for not tapdancing fast enough as I tried desperately to meet her needs.

But I couldn't stand to see Meesha upset, so without considering the implications, I blurted, "I'll . . . watch . . . Lola . . . temporarily . . . until you find someone else . . ."

That someone else became me. Meesha and I co-parented Lola for the next ten years.

Despite my reservations, and despite Lola's relentless high-pitched barking that hit notes that would've made Mariah Carey envious, this fawn-colored pip-squeak nuzzled her way into my heart. It happened on the day she jumped on my lap and looked up at me with her penetrating gaze. It started off as a staring contest—she was a champion gaze-holder, like no other dog, or person, I'd ever known. I don't know how this reverie happened, but a transmission of love wound its way through the cosmos and into her tiny body, shot through her eyes into mine, ricocheted around, and blasted my heart open.

I'd never felt such love. Shaking from the impact, out of my mouth popped, "Lola, you're my portal to the Universe, aren't you?" And with that, her work was done. She curled into a ball, closed her intense eyes, and took a nap in my lap. Like I'd been shot through the heart by Cupid, I was never the same.

For the next ten years, she became my constant companion and fellow peanut butter freak, her body a part of my own. Wherever I went, she followed, and I didn't mind. Her high-pitched yipes continued, but they'd stop the moment she was nestled by my side. She became my writing partner and muse, and I thanked her for the daily and hourly hits of the sweetest oxytocin surges she inspired while being attached at my hip.

Over the years, despite the love showered on her by my family, when Dana and I traveled for business, Lola's life force diminished. In fact, several times, when Meesha was unable to watch her, pet sitters reported they didn't think she'd survive the night. But the moment Lola, Meesha, and I were reunited, she'd resume being as feisty as ever, running like fire in the wind, gobbling her food with gusto. But as the years marched on, as happens to all of us, she began showing signs of age.

As the blur of cataracts clouded her vision, her declining health made me strangely grateful for the COVID years, because as we sheltered in place, I was able to be with her as she became more brittle. When she was no longer able to walk, I became her arms and legs, holding her to eat, drink, tinkle, and do her other outdoor doggie business.

And then came the night I knew would be the last. Growing old is one thing, but suffering (whimpering, unable to eat or drink) is another. I tossed and turned—then out of nowhere, a dream took me on Lola's tour de force behind the scenes. I gasped as I beheld her melding into shooting stars, swirling planets, Venus and Mars. The faint outline of her frame blurred like an extinguished candle in the night, like a sandcastle yielding to a toppling wave, a firework's grand finale as she dropped her charade.

Here's how I OGLE'd it:

O: *What is the Offending behavior and/or situation?*

Originally, Meesha's landlord gave Lola the boot. Next was taking in a dog that I didn't particularly want to co-parent. Then, after I was struck my love's lightning bolt, and a decade-long lovefest, she died. My day-in, day-out companion, around whom my life revolved, is no longer physical, and it sucks. I'm heartbroken, and I miss her physical presence and her sweet, demanding essence. The ache of Lola's absence can't be healed with platitudes or the Band-Aid of sympathetic attitudes.

G: *What is Good about that offending behavior and/or situation?*

Although I'll miss her every day, I'm aware we all have an expiration date. We're all cosmic beings, none of us true earthlings. All of us are angels here for a while, taking a spin around the mortal turnstile. I'm grateful for this dream—for it healed my soul, reminding me that beneath her dog suit, she is perfect and whole, stardust busting at the seams, barely containing the galaxy behind the scenes, trying hard to keep her light ratcheted in, belted tight, buckled in.

What's great about the dream is that my awareness of her cosmic identity does not feel theoretical or hypothetical. I saw, with my very own dreaming eyes, what's hidden to most; I watched my dog become a holy ghost. I glimpsed the Universe within her skin, the grandeur beneath her fur, as she blurred into the multiverse from whence she came . . . until at last, she swirled into a galactic (dog) star.

L: *How am I peering into the Looking Glass (mirror)?*

Death, in a dream and in waking reality, I believe, is about great change, an opportunity to let go of outworn costumes. In the looking glass, the Lola part of me passed away. This marks the end and, simultaneously, a beginning of a new chapter in my life. Perhaps this is an opportunity to become a lighter, brighter version of myself too.

Maybe none of us are who we think we are, instead all just fractals of the same star. Perhaps in order to play the game of being earthlings, we all slip on a suit, ten times too small, and join the festivities at the grand masquerade ball, squeezing into the belief we're mere mortals and our animals mere pets. We forget that we're heavenly creatures playing the role of paupers, giants playing the role of dwarfs, lions playing the role of kittens.

But I wonder if it's possible to behold the truth while still on earth. Why else would we opt to be birthed into this life with amnesia, without anesthesia? I suppose we do wake up, in rare moments, from time to time. We fumble, bumble, and stumble until, with no reason or rhyme, we lock eyes with a being we love . . . and remember the truth of each other, and of ourselves, and in so doing, we take the Holy Grail off the shelf.

E: *How will I allow this situation to Elevat me? What Elevated action will I take?*

I remember that life happens when we're making other plans—and the best way to make God laugh is to tell her my plans. Despite appearances, first impressions, and my initial resistance to her, Lola became one of the greatest blessings I've ever had in my life. Because of her, I'm more apt to suspend judgment of the "gift dogs" (both people and canines) I might otherwise I've looked in the mouth and, instead, I've become enriched by the bounty of their strange beauty.

Besides wanting to love like Lola did, my elevated action is to continue not taking my dreams lying down, to refrain from casting off my nocturnal visions as mere mental meanderings of a sleep-deprived mind, spiritual fluff to leave behind. I'm allowing this dream to have its way with me, overriding morbid default thoughts of death and dying. Instead of falling off heartache's cliff, I will stay attuned to the same universal love Lola transmitted to me throughout the years—even though her physical presence is now absent.

This dream is the touchstone I hold, especially when I pad across the cold, empty hardwood floor by my bed. Instead of being filled with dread, I remember to dive into the stream of my dream to snap out of heartbreak's trance . . . and allow the warm breeze of cherished memories to dance across my mind.

So, it turns out, this unassuming Chiweenie with a high-pitched squeak, in addition to being my constant companion and fellow peanut butter freak, was a cosmic being, all along.

My elevated action is the constant remembering of Lola removing her dog suit. Forever immortal in my eye, Lola became the universal sky.

Hot Air

Mexico

*To be fully alive, fully human, and completely awake
is to be continually thrown out of the nest. To live fully is to be
always in no-man's-land, to experience each moment
as completely new and fresh. To live is to be willing
to die over and over again.*

PEMA CHÖDRÖN

Enjoying the expansive vista of the desert below and sky beyond the rattan basket, my five-person group and I were like babies whisked through the air in the beak of a massive stork. Flying three thousand feet in the air, above the clouds, beneath a rainbow-colored hot-air balloon, we were giggly as school kids, oohing and ahhing at the rosy hue that, like spun sugar, stretched across the morning sky.

Then, just as our collective joy threatened to shatter the sound barrier, a storm cloud darkened our pilot's formerly cheery face.

Thirty minutes earlier, on the ground before takeoff, in her black puffer jacket and gray fingerless gloves, Sylvia was a study in competence. I didn't mind her bragging about flying hot-air balloons for ten years, with over a thousand successful flights under her belt. Our all-female group nodded, impressed, agreeing we were in good hands. But after a half hour of flight, Sylvia's confidence, like the sandbags she dropped out of the basket at liftoff, seemed to have plummeted as well.

I spoke a decent amount of Spanish, but I'd never heard the words Sylvia spouted into her CB radio: "Zoholo-something." My stomach sank with the realization that something was wrong.

On all my dozen previous group expeditions in Teotihuacán, Mexico, we'd never taken a hot-air balloon ride. These five-day spiritual pilgrimages were an attempt to replicate, in some small way, what the spiritual aspirants of the ancient Toltec mystery school did over a lifetime. The practices were earth based, including miles of walking, hiking, climbing pyramids, not to mention meditating in the dirt, on the rocks—in an attempt to stay grounded while availing ourselves of the heavenly wisdom so palpable in this place. Up until this moment, our trip had been seamless.

Normally when I facilitated these excursions, I stuck to a tried-and-true, boots-on-the-ground process I learned when I was a student. But this time, the group became enchanted during morning yoga, gazing in the sunrise at the hot-air balloons, which were like a party gliding through the cotton-candy clouds. Someone exclaimed in tree pose, "I wish we could join them!"

I am typically one for adventure, but when it involves a group I'm responsible for, I lean conservatively. But I got swept up in the enthusiasm that followed, and I admitted I also felt a bit of FOMO watching those bright balloons confetti-ing the clouds. Fine. Let's do it. What could it hurt?

So, before the crack of another day's dawn, while the sky was still inky and the air was still frosty, a van picked up our barely coherent bunch and whisked us to hot-air-balloon headquarters.

In the wild blue yonder, Sylvia, our formerly smiley pilot, grimaced with eyebrows knitted in a V, like the formation of the birds we'd just passed. Alarm bells rang through me, but I looked away, trying to convince myself I was overdramatizing the situation. *We're going to be OK. She's done this a thousand times. It's highly unlikely this will be the one time she isn't successful.*

I joined the group singing a mash-up of songs from *The Wizard of Oz*: "Somewhere Over the Rainbow," "We're Off to See the Wizard," "Follow the Yellow Brick Road." Until someone noticed the wind had gotten stronger and we were zipping quickly through the sky, no longer gliding. Someone else noticed there were no other hot-air balloons anywhere near us, when we'd been part of a bouquet of them just moments before.

I turned my attention back to Sylvia, who was busily cranking up the indigo flames, like a dragon feeding a hungry ghost, creating an upsurge lift. If I could just decode what Zoholo-something meant, maybe I could figure out what was going on. Before I could give that more thought, yet another surprise distracted me.

I leaned over and whispered to my friend Nancy, a gorgeous brunette with a quick wit, "Am I crazy, or is that a giraffe down there?" She responded, "Yep, and look over there! It's a camel!" At first, I couldn't see it, but as I squinted, it came into focus. Yes, it was definitely a giraffe. What in God's name was a giraffe doing there? Had we fallen into the twilight zone, slipped through the cracks, gotten carried away in a slipstream of wind just for us, or all of all above?

Then someone else spouted, "Is that an elephant?" Someone else yelled out, "Are those caribou?" In unison, as if everyone received the same memo, they all started chanting, "Lions and Tigers and Bears, Oh My!"

Then Nancy laughed. "Wouldn't it be funny if we landed in the midst of the wild animals?"

Just then, it dawned on me what Zoholo-something meant. It was a zoo—or maybe more accurately, a wild animal park, and we were beelining right toward it!

Panicked, Sylvia turned all her dials, switches, and knobs. No longer singing, four sets of wide eyes were suddenly on me. Apparently the alarm bells I thought I'd kept on the down low weren't down low enough. Everyone asked, "What's Sylvia saying? What's going on?"

As the group's leader, even though I had no idea what to do, I tried to sound as just-the-facts-ma'am as the weather forecaster on TV reporting partly cloudy, chance of showers. "She's telling us to brace ourselves. Hold tight to the side of the basket and bend your knees to absorb the impact."

As we careened closer to the earth, way too fast, Sylvia lifted her shoulders, looked at me with an apologetic *Lo siento* (I'm sorry). I held my breath and sent silent prayers to all my angels and Toltec gods, including Our Lady of Guadalupe.

I squeezed my eyes shut and next thing I felt was a *smack* as we hit the ground. The next thing I knew, I was pitched out of the basket and crawling from beneath a puppy pile of legs, arms, elbows, and torsos. Woozy, shocked, and delirious, our group was thankfully an optimistic bunch who focused on gratitude for us all being OK versus freaking out in panic over having crash-landed in a wild animal park.

I lifted myself, wobbly, to standing and brushed myself off. As my eyes panned from the ground to the sky, I beheld the most gorgeous yellow-and-brown-splotched giraffe. I stared, agog, into his giant pools for eyes, rimmed with a curtain of eyelashes. My hands instinctively assumed a prayer position in front of my heart as he ambled closer to me.

For a moment, my mind shifted away from fretting about how my group and I would get out of this wild animal sanctuary, and my memory flung me back like a slingshot to a nonviolent communication (NVC) course I'd taken a decade before. I remembered the way the grand poohbah of NVC, Marshall Rosenberg, cleverly used hand puppets. A jackal was his metaphor of violent (critical, reactive, hurtful) communication, versus the giraffe, who symbolized nonviolent (responsible, empowering, respectful) communication. He said, "Giraffes are wise, gentle, with a sky-high perspective, as well as having the largest heart—relative to their size—of any land mammal."[37]

Over the years since I'd taken that course, when I'd find myself tempted to be a jackal, I'd contemplate, "What would the giraffe do? What would he say (if he could speak human)?" And I'd do my best to course correct in a way that would make Rosenberg—and the giraffe—proud.

Without consciously realizing it, I projected a combination of Gandhi, Buddha, Mother Theresa, and Martin Luther King Jr. onto this real-life giraffe and thus did not respond with the fear I probably should have.

The giraffe must've inferred that I was available for a more up-close-and-personal connection. His long, long legs gracefully moved toward me, until there we stood, face-to-face, making eye contact like star-crossed lovers. I stood in stunned stillness, completely at his mercy. I took in a deep breath as this twenty-foot-tall giant sniffed the crown of my head, then kissed me on my forehead. Then, like in a love-'em-and-leave-'em encounter, he turned and walked away and left me breathless, but with a smile nothing would be able to erase.

Nancy fumbled for her phone to capture the moment but couldn't snap the photo fast enough. Then everyone, as if in hive mind, grabbed their phones to document this happening. Shouting ensued, panicked voices from the men in khaki who ran the wild animal sanctuary, "Deja de tomar fotos. Las luces intermitentes asustan a los animales!" (Stop taking photos. The flashing lights scare the animals!)

While Sylvia got scolded, a convertible jeep barreled in, encircling us with a plume of dust; a khaki-clad driver gestured for us to quickly jump in. As he skidded with us off the premises, we discovered the proximity of the lions: less than a football throw from where we crashed. Only a flimsy chain-link fence separated us from them. With just a slight change in wind, we could've landed not with the giraffes, camels, and caribou but among the lions!

Here's how I OGLE'd it:

O: *What is the Offending behavior and/or situation?*

Even though it turned out to be one of the most magical experiences of my life, had I been given the choice ahead of time, knowing we would crash in the middle of a wild animal sanctuary, scaredy-cat that I am, I would've said, "Hell to the no."

G: *What is Good about that offending behavior and/or situation?*

Even though Sylvia was unable to keep us from crashing among the animals, she was competent enough to ensure we survived. Besides the fact that none of us died or got injured or eaten by a lion, what was good about this situation was this most extraordinary communion with that beautiful giraffe, whom the driver said was named Luis Miguel (after the great Mexican artist.)

L: *How am I peering into the Looking Glass (mirror)?*

Like the wind and Sylvia, whose job was to keep us in the air and ensure a smooth, safe landing, the fine print in the contract we signed said something along the lines of "We are not responsible for injury or death." I, too, only want kumbaya-level harmony on my watch, but it doesn't always go that way. It wasn't my fault, as much as it wasn't Sylvia's fault, that the winds of fate had a different plan for us. It's what happens when you take a risk: sometimes it works, and sometimes it doesn't. But as they say in Spanish, vale la pena— it's (usually) worth it.

Standing toe to hoof with Luis Miguel gave me the blessing of peering into the looking glass of a towering yet gentle presence. I also aspire to stand tall, like him, in my (spiritual) stature. This tête-à-tête was worth falling from the sky for.

E: *How will I allow this situation to Elevate me? What Elevated action will I take?*

If you've been reading my stories, you might be detecting a theme: I'm no stranger to the best-laid plans being blown to smithereens by the winds of change. But luckily, so far (knock wood), I'm still here, alive and well to tell the tale and to alchemize the tragic into magic. As an optimist, I expect things to work out because (despite the stories chronicled in this book) they usually do unfold with unnoteworthy grace.

I could say this crash made me not want to ever do anything crazy like that again, but I'd be full of hot air—because the next year when I returned to Teotihuacán, I was right up there again.

I didn't see Sylvia and didn't ask for her. I'm relieved (although, to be honest, slightly disappointed) to report, the second ride was without incident, taking off and landing exactly according to plan.

My elevated perspective was to map Luis Miguel's high-vibe point of view onto my own brain—especially when things fall apart—because that's when the most life-changing blessings reveal themselves. They're the people we meet and the creatures we encounter when we've fallen off the beaten track who often change the trajectory of our lives for the better.

One of my favorite teachings from the Senoi dream tribe is their perspective on falling dreams. Most dream cultures believe falling is akin to failing, often a result of being overwhelmed and ungrounded. However, the Senoi believe we have falling spirits who are calling us into our depths. The goal in these dreams is not to avoid falling but to learn to fall well. I believe this is not only true for our nighttime dreams but for our waking dreams too.

Later that afternoon, after I was back at our compound, I called my husband and confessed, "Our hot-air balloon crashed. We're all fine. But you should know, I met a tall, handsome, brown-eyed stranger named Luis Miguel. We kissed in the meadow, and I'm in love. Don't be jealous that I look up to him. I can't help it; he's a giraffe."

I Need a Hug

Southern California

A hug a day keeps the demons at bay.

PROVERB

"I'm not here to have a session with you," confessed the sweating man in my living room, my new client, who reminded me of the photo on a wanted poster for a serial killer. "I'm here because I didn't know how else to get close to you . . . and this seemed like the only way."

The man I'll call Jeremy had booked a spiritual counseling session with me. On the phone he said he had gotten my number from our church's Sunday bulletin. Several of my clients had come from there, so I thought nothing of it. Until I met him.

There I sat in my living room/office with this strange man with long, dark curls wrangled by a fedora. He was shifty, with beady eyes barely able to make eye contact. I felt a sickening, queasy feeling while sitting across from him.

My mind flashed back to the practitioner meeting I attended at church the week before. Every month we spiritual counselors (practitioners) met for supervision and peer support for help with our clients, as well as for issues in our own lives. At this meeting, one of my dearest colleagues, Deanna, who was normally calm, powerful, and self-possessed, was visibly shaken. Her voice trembled as she shared with the group that she had to file a restraining order against a new client who was sexually obsessed with her and not respecting her boundaries.

For a reason I can't recall, I had to leave the meeting early, before I found out this man's name or what he looked like. A jolt of panic now ripped through me as I wondered if this man seated before me was the very stalker about whom my friend had been trying to warn me. A second bolt of lightning zapped me when I realized I'd done my presession protocol: I'd shut off my phone and hung a do-not-disturb sign outside my locked door. *I'm an idiot!*

I made it so easy for someone to rape or murder me. I was the perfect sitting duck. All he had to do was call and schedule an appointment; I had no screening mechanism back then. I became furious at myself for being so stupid.

Then my client continued, "I saw you in church giving someone a hug, and I wished it was me. But since I didn't know you, I knew I'd never get a hug like that. Then, as I read the bulletin, I noticed you were a practitioner, and your phone number was right there . . ."

In that moment, I became aware of the tug-of-war between two distinct aspects of myself. On one side there was the spiritual counselor and hypnotherapist who'd been earning her healing stripes over the last few years. On the other end of the rope was the fear-based me, who was still carting around PTSD baggage from past assaults (some of which I've shared in this book). The movie montage played, flashing images of so many other threats to my safety, including years before when another male client exposed himself (not his heart but his manhood) and then began calling me in the middle of the night and threatening to come over, which eventually resulted in me changing my phone number and even moving.

But somehow I knew, if my fear took over, it might trigger this man's aggression and make things worse. He was stronger than me and could hurt me. So, if ever there was a moment to put my spiritual skills to the test, this was it.

Despite my horror, my PTSD, and a lifetime of feeling unsafe with (strange) men, like a mother lifting a car to save her child, I conjured all my light, summoned my angels, and deliberately stepped into the highest field of love I could find. I turned on my God firehose, and I blasted him with prayer: "You may think you came here for a hug, but I believe the only reason you would feel the need to lie about your intent for coming to see me is because there's some part of you, like in all of us humans, that believes you're not good enough—that you're somehow cut off from God, separate from the good and fulfilling things in this world. Well, I'm here to tell you the truth is you are at one with God. God is your life and substance. You have never been separated from God's love for one second in your whole life. Just because you have thoughts that tell you otherwise doesn't make them true."

By the end of the hour, he was in tears, and I'd never felt like a more powerful vessel of love and truth. I walked him to the door then hugged him, as I did with all my clients. I wished him well, and I watched him walk down the stairs, climb into his car, and drive away.

The moment his red taillights receded from sight, the fear I'd been keeping at bay broke loose. I removed the do-not-disturb sign (since I was now disturbed), slammed my door, then locked and deadbolted myself inside. Sliding down the closed door into a heap, my whole body was wracked with sobs.

The next day, Jeremy left a voice mail saying how much he loved our session and asked if he could book another one as soon as possible. I stared at the phone for what seemed like an hour. *If I am truly the spiritual counselor I aspire to be, I should be able to work with anyone. Am I a wimp—a spiritual baby—for not wanting to see him?*

Dizzy with confusion, unable to figure out what to do, I dialed Nirvana, my practitioner, and filled him in on the situation. At the conclusion of our call, Nirvana said he'd be willing to take my client off my hands, and a deep relief washed over me.

I returned Jeremy's call. I told him I was glad he enjoyed our session. But going forward, I was referring him to my practitioner, whom I thought would be a better fit for him. After all, Nirvana was the one who taught me everything I knew. "If you want to grow spiritually, you will reach out to Nirvana. He's expecting your call."

Despite Jeremy's pleading with me for another session, my boundaries were ironclad. I would not be a fool again.

With my perfect solution, I thought the case was closed. Especially since I made a promise to myself: should I ever take on a new (male) client, I would alert my husband to check on me after the hour and keep my phone on and my door unlocked. But the next Sunday at church, instead of sitting up front where I normally did, I sat in the back row, wearing dark shades. I didn't want to see, or be seen by, anyone . . . and most especially, I didn't want to hug anybody.

A few days later, for the first time in years, the depression and anxiety I'd been able to keep on the down low came out from hiding like a wound-up jack-in-the-box and was now running the show. Paranoia set in, as I felt I could no longer trust people. I second-guessed smiling strangers I passed on the street who said hello. In the back of my mind, I'd think, *Sure, you appear friendly, but underneath your facade, you're probably a psycho stalker.* It no longer felt safe to walk through life with an open heart. To cope, I shrank, became a smaller, more defensive, cynical version of myself.

It became painful simply to live in my skin. The worst thing was I had nothing to justify why I felt so unsafe in the world. If a violation had taken place while I was loitering in a dark alley, it would've been horrible but not nearly as much as it being associated with my church, the place I went to be spiritually and emotionally naked, to let go of the stress of the world. I felt like he'd ripped away my safe harbor. I couldn't stop feeling like I understood (to some degree) the trauma of someone who'd been raped at church. Not only was there a violation, but the biggest offense was he took church away from me.

This shut-down version of me eked out a semblance of life for another month, during which time I was plagued with nightmares of Jeremy being the dangerous stalker for whom my non-wimpy friend had gotten the restraining order. Not only did I spot Jeremy at church a few times but it seemed everywhere I went, Jeremy look-alikes cropped up, triggering mini-anxiety attacks each time.

And then the day came when I could take no more. I was surrounded by red, green, and silver holiday lights and instrumental Christmas music piping into our local Barnes & Noble. Normally I was a cheery Christmas person. But this year, all the eggnog in the world couldn't maneuver the boulder from my heart. Then I saw, yet again, another Jeremy look-alike, in the aisle next to me. I had no idea where or what book my husband had gotten engrossed in; I didn't want to look for him and risk being spotted by Jeremy (or his twin). So, as irony would have it, I crouched down in the self-help section and hid. *This has got to stop!* I dropped to the ground and sat cross-legged, whipped out my journal from my purse, and OGLE'd Jeremy with the intent to exorcise him from my life, once and for all.

O: *What is the Offending behavior and/or situation?*

Jeremy lied. He booked a session with me under false pretenses. He terrified me and for the last few months robbed me of my open heart, my church, and my ability to freely hug people.

And what if he had been a psychopath and put my life at stake?

G: *What is Good about that offending behavior and/or situation?*

Even though Jeremy lied about his intent for the session, he came clean within minutes of being in front of me. All he claimed to want was a hug. If that was true, then what he wanted was inspired by an inherently good and life-serving impulse. To want to hug means he is healthy enough to be attuned to the natural human impulse for connection.

The session with him gave me the rare opportunity to discover my ability to set aside my small-mindedness and fears while proving to myself I had it in me to conjure a highly charged, tapped-in message, even under duress.

L: *How am I peering into the Looking Glass (mirror)?*

I wasn't honest with him either. I didn't feel safe to tell Jeremy how terrified I felt. He didn't do anything to me . . . but tell me the truth. He came into my home, sat in a chair, and told me he wanted a hug. I'm the one who projected murder, mayhem, and the stuff of horror movies onto him. I'm the one who allowed this incident to traumatize me. So, who's the real psycho?

Like Jeremy, I also have a need for connection. Just a month of being hug deprived was enough to nearly cause irreparable damage to my soul. It was like hiding a flower in a dark basement and wondering why its petals wilted.

In fact, I could turn the sermon I gave Jeremy on myself and remind myself I am at one with the whole of life, not broken in any way. If I can remember to remember my intrinsic relationship with God, the Universe, and all of humanity, I might be able to restore myself to my formerly openhearted state.

E: *How will I allow this situation to Elevate me? What Elevated action will I take?*

I'm known for teaching that a nightmare is an unfinished dream. We can pretend our shadows don't exist, slam the door, and lock ourselves away from them. But I believe if we don't alchemize them, they will continue to haunt us, and our life force will shrink.

As is the case every time I OGLE, I'm blown away at the relief I feel when I recognize the behavior I fear, dislike, or resist in someone else is within me. The alchemy comes when I swallow the bitter pill and realize the devil is not at large, running around outside me. The entire hologram of life is within me. There is no shadow from which I need to hide. Relating to, recognizing, and embracing my own fear-based thoughts, as strange as it may seem, is the only way this prodigal daughter has ever found her way back to being enfolded by the loving arms of the Universe—and no one but me can take that away from me.

It turns out, Jeremy was not the man for whom my practitioner friend had to get a restraining order. He was just a lonely guy who needed a hug.

Infinite Pie

Southern California

Success makes so many people hate you. I wish it wasn't that way. It would be wonderful to enjoy success without seeing envy in the eyes of those around you.

—MARILYN MONROE

In the midst of one of my many dark nights of the soul in my youth, triggered by an extreme drought in my then nearly nonexistent acting career, I enrolled in a weekend-long world-renowned transformational seminar along with my boyfriend at the time. Rumor had it, we'd come out of the program more successful than we were when we went in.

My boyfriend was a fellow actor, a tall, dark, and brooding martial artist I'll call Karate Guy. We were both ambitious and, honestly (and embarrassingly), a bit competitive with each other about who would make their mark on Hollywood first. Neither of us were anywhere close to making a smudge, much less anything resembling a mark. Sure, we'd both gotten a smattering of parts, big roles in low-budget indie productions and bit parts in larger productions. But most of the time, rejection was my constant companion, and my fragile ego was hanging off a cliff by a frayed spiderweb thread. I was open to any miracle the acting gods could toss my way, which was why I decided to be proactive and dedicate a weekend to self-reflection, under the klieg lights of this popular seminar.

The workshop was emotionally and spiritually grueling but ultimately insightful and inspiring, despite the long hours and rare bathroom breaks. Before the completion, to keep the momentum alive in our lives beyond the castle walls of the course, the instructor strongly urged us to be accountable, to meet in person with two other participants for five weeks. In these follow-up sessions, we agreed to discuss our goals and support each other to stay aligned with the breakthroughs we had, while integrating the principles we learned in the workshop.

As I scanned the sea of people in the massive ballroom, I felt a full-body *yes!* to this commitment. Such an incredible assortment of humans, of all shapes, sizes, races, and ages—I marveled at my eclectic and interesting comrades and couldn't wait to see who the third person would be to join my boyfriend and me. Then I spotted the only person I prayed would not join us.

Of course, as fate would have it, much to the chagrin of my ego, of the hundred-plus souls at the workshop, the seminar leader assigned Karate Guy and me with guess who. The third member of our group was not a hairy beast but the most gorgeous young starlet I'd ever seen—on screen or off.

My frayed thread snapped, and my heart plummeted. Why, in God's name, did the seminar leader partner us with her?

I grew up in an all-female house (except my dad) and, thus, was raised with a healthier-than-normal dose of girl power. As the eldest of five sisters, I was taught to support all women as though they were my sisters. I credited, at least partially, being a true girl's girl for why I'd always been lucky with girlfriends.

Of course I'd felt the pang of jealousy a few times before, but I had always easily and quickly brushed it off, returning back to the empowering state of "as one is lifted, all are lifted." But, come on, Universe, this was too much.

This young starlet with whom I was forced to spend the next five intimate weeks was everything and had everything I thought I should be and have but wasn't and didn't. Not only was her career taking off but she was literally the toast of Hollywood, with her gorgeous face plastered on the cover of every major magazine and billboard. Not only was she a perfect ten, beyond lovely, funny, charming, intelligent, with the most adorable figure, but she was nearly ten years younger, and at least ten pounds lighter, than me. If all that wasn't enough, I could've sworn I saw sparks flying between her and Karate Guy. I took a deep breath, plastered on the world's fakest smile, and did everything in my power to refrain from spewing green pea soup as my head spun, à la Linda Blair in *The Exorcist*.

At our first meeting, over pie and coffee, the three of us cozied into a booth at our local Denny's. Starlet removed her shades and looked at me like an orphan being reunited with her lost mother. She was clueless about the fact that I was doing everything in my power not to run from her like I would a burning building.

Sipping coffee, she opened up candidly about her struggle with fame and fortune and all the attention she was getting—in fact, she had to sit with her back to the rest of the restaurant patrons, so, God forbid, no one would spot her and call the paparazzi. I duct taped my mouth to repress the urge to scream, *I'd sell my soul to have your problems!*

But it was when she shared about her goals to make even bigger movies, with even bigger costars and even bigger directors, that I finally understood what the saying "I'm beside myself" meant: because even though my body was seated on the squeaky booth between Starlet and Karate Guy, I could feel the rest of me slipping away.

Relief set in when Karate Guy took his turn to share. Thank God, because I knew I could never open my mouth, much less my heart, and share about my teensy-weensy pathetic acting goals, out loud, to her. If she had had the decency to let her starlight shine from a safe distance, I would've been fine. But the fact that this goddess had the audacity to float down from Mount Olympus and plop herself down in the booth between Karate Guy and me was too much. To be up close and personal with this level of royalty left me feeling like a groveling pauper, of the Charles Dickens variety. I know, I know, compare despair, but I couldn't help it.

As she nodded in support of Karate Guy's goals, my inner critic grabbed a bullhorn, turned up the volume, and berated me: *You're a fat, old, dried-up, ugly, worthless fool. Why don't you just go away so Starlet and Karate Guy can make out already.*"

As the warning signs of a panic attack rumbled—airways constricting, heart fluttering like a hummingbird's wings—I accessed my inner actress, B-level though she was, and excused myself to the ladies' room.

But instead of going into the bathroom, I dropped a quarter into an available payphone (this was before the days of cell phones) and sent smoke signals to Nirvana, my spiritual coach.

Thank the Lord he answered and had a spare moment to hear me spew my dilemma and need for a miracle right then and right there. Then, in his inimitable fashion, Nirvana walloped me with a spiritual two-by-four. "The reason you're in so much pain is because when you look at her, all you see is your failure. You've made up a story that there is a finite amount of pie, and since she has such a big piece, there are only crumbs left for you. That's ridiculous. Knock it off. You know there's infinite pie for all of us, even if your pie slice is cut a little differently than everyone else's."

I gulped and pressed the receiver into my ear to not miss a word above the clanking of plates in the background. He continued, "It's done unto you as you believe . . . so what if you made up a story that you are lucky to have Starlet in your life because she's giving you a personal backstage pass to the success you will one day have, in your own way? Go ahead and try it now."

I closed my eyes and envisioned her gorgeous, smiling face, honey hair, and seafoam eyes. I told myself she was a catalyst, a reminder of the pie I would one day have. Even though it felt like a stretch, and I wasn't 100 percent convinced I wasn't just rationalizing, in spite of myself, my pulse calmed, the panic receded, and the tumbleweed of self-loathing was replaced by a calm, cool breeze.

I thanked Nirvana, and with my head (mostly) screwed back on, I walked back to the table. Starlet and Karate Guy were so wrapped in their lively conversation, they didn't seem to notice I'd been gone.

I felt differently. Something had shifted. Even with the two of them making googly eyes at each other, I was no longer plagued with the jealousy I'd been debilitated by just minutes before. Instead, I felt a tiny flame of hope in my heart giving me the message there might just be room for me in this world. Maybe I wasn't so much of a has-been (or a never-was) after all. Maybe I just hadn't come into my stride . . . yet.

For a blissful moment, I stopped seeing her as a pie hog. No longer a threat, the scales fell from my eyes, and I could see that this beautiful young woman needed a big sister. She took another sip of coffee and nibble of her own piece of her pecan pie (mine was still totally intact) and turned the light of her attention to me. Through teary eyes, she confessed she came to the workshop because she was losing it. Even though she'd never been more outwardly successful, her family and all her trusted friends had revealed their true, greedy colors. She'd never felt more alone in the world. I felt guilty when she said, "You guys," meaning me and Karate Guy, "are the only ones I can trust."

From that moment on, thanks to the much-needed spiritual kick in the pants from Nirvana, I had the bandwidth available in my heart to truly listen to her and be a space of genuine support, not the fake kind.

We met a few more times, even after our fifth session was complete, until she left on location for her next film. As we all hugged goodbye, she shared about how much she'd grown during our Denny's sessions. I couldn't bring myself to tell her how profoundly she'd contributed to my own growth by being a symbol of hope for my slice of the infinite pie I would one day have.

Over the following days, weeks, months, and years, here's how I OGLE'd it:

O: *What is the Offending behavior and/or situation?*

Starlet was a thousand times more successful than I was, and her presence made me feel like a lowly wannabe loser.

G: *What is Good about that offending behavior and/or situation?*

Thanks to Nirvana and my willingness to reach for a higher perspective, I was able to have a breakthrough that's carried with me throughout my life. It's turned out to be an elixir for me, one I've been able to share with others when they're ravaged by the green-eyed monster.

L: *How am I peering into the Looking Glass (mirror)?*

Shadow work is never easy—especially, as strange as it seems, when it comes to the light shadow. What I learned later in my dream studies is most of us think of the shadow as a scary or awful energy we reject because we unconsciously think of it as beneath us. But a light shadow is just as painful and rejectable. Looking into the mirror of someone we put on a pedestal, above us, is just as much of an illusion as is putting someone beneath us. Both experiences leave us feeling cut off and separate from ourselves and from the life force of the Universe. The simple (but not easy) act of embracing the being in the mirror (energetically lighter or heavier than us) gives us an infusion of spiritual rocket fuel so we can blast into our place in the spotlight of our own lives.

E: *How will I allow this situation to Elevate me? What Elevated action will I take?*

A few weeks later, practicing what Nirvana preached, as I drove the streets of Hollywood and looked up to see Starlet smiling down on me from lofty billboards. I forced myself to take a breath and send her a silent *Thank you*, for being a catalyst, for pointing the way, and for showing me that, although our paths are different, there's pie enough for me. As I did this, a neuro-network began to fuse, causing me to glimpse a vision of my own potential success—even though I had no idea what it might be, when it might be, or how it would unfold.

All these years later, it turns out I did come into my own success, not as an actor, but in the role much closer to home and closer to my soul, Doctor Dream. Nirvana was right in that my path did unfold incredibly different from Starlet's. And I wouldn't change a thing.

In fact, as synchronicity would have it, years later, in 2021, I wrote the book *Luminous Humanness: 365 Ways to Go, Grow & Glow to Make It Your Best Year Yet.* In this book, there's an affirmative message for each day of the year. The day after I wrote "Infinite Pie," on February 9, 2022, I was surprised at the synchronicity when I read the message in my book, inspired by those Denny's meetings with Starlet twenty-seven years before:

February 9th
As They Are Lifted, You Are Lifted
Anyone's breakthrough is everyone's breakthrough. When you witness a coworker's success, a friend's financial windfall, a family member fall in love, or even a celebrity in the media living la vida loca, say to yourself, "Spot it, you got it." In other words, consider those who appear more accomplished are in your life to be your north star, pointing you toward what's possible for you, in your unique expression. As you become more adept at celebrating other people's wins as if they were your own, you become an attractor beam for more good fortune in your life. And, when you come into your own success, there will be no need to sabotage or downplay it. When you dedicate your good fortune to inspiring others, as you've been inspired, you will light the way for others to live their dreams.

Affirmation: I dedicate my windfalls of success to uplifting the world.[38]

In other words, there's an infinite pie—more than enough for all of us to feast to our heart's content.

She Speaks Whale

Northern California

Don't you hear it? she asked and I shook my head no and then she started to dance and suddenly there was music everywhere and it went on for a very long time and when I finally found words all I could say was thank you.

BRIAN ANDREAS

Three days after my dear friend Gypsy died, I was exhausted on every level from nonstop crying, interrupted only by episodes of vomiting, thoroughly wrung out.

For over a year since she'd received her cancer diagnosis, I'd been holding back my sadness, fear, and heartbreak in an attempt to be the rock of Gyp-raltar, a sturdy, safe space for Gypsy to lean on during the most difficult time of her life.

I pulled a card from my *Hero's Journey Dream Oracle Deck* and demanded that she communicate with me: "Gypsy, where are you, and what are you doing?"

The card I pulled in response to the question read: "Whale of a Time."

Really? God, I hoped it was true.

I met her twenty-seven years before, in December of 1993, in an AA meeting in L.A. Yes, I know, I'm blowing our anonymity. At this point, I think she'd be OK with that, since she and I both turned out not to be true alcoholics—and she no longer has an ego . . . or a body, for that matter.

At the end of the meeting, the speaker asked the newcomers to stand. Since I was a seasoned twelve-stepper, having been around for a whopping two weeks at that point, I was relieved this command no longer applied to me. Instead, my then therapist/sponsor instructed me to write my name and phone number on slips of paper and give them to ten female newcomers at every meeting I attended. I knew one I would give my number to: Gypsy, the waif with long, black hair, a pale face, and two oceans for eyes I'd seen earlier. She seemed to be holding on to life by a whisper.

After the meeting, I handed her my piece of paper as we walked outside. There, she lit a cigarette and shared with me why she was so shaken. Two weeks earlier, her two-year-old baby girl, Hillary, passed away in the night of SIDS (sudden infant death syndrome).

I instinctively wrapped my arms around her in the tightest koala bear hug, and a bolt of destiny struck my heart, and I made an unspoken promise to be there for her as she navigated how to live after such an unthinkable loss.

I was so delighted the next morning when my phone rang. It was Gypsy reaching out for support, having no idea the level of turmoil I was in. But the fact that she called me for help lifted me to a higher place in myself where I could access wisdom I didn't know I had. She had no idea how much she helped me in a way no therapy, book, shaman, or medication could.

Starting that day, we became attached at the soul, spending nearly every day together, over lunch and twelve-step meetings, talking late into the night about music, spirituality, and past lives. She read me her tear-jerking, haunting, and lyrical poetry which inspired me to pick up a pen and write. Before we could blink, we were crafting songs together, and our creativity became the life raft that kept us both afloat, out of the swamp of survival mode and in the river of thriving.

She insisted on driving us on road trips. She'd take me cruising in her blue Camaro, Dolphinmobile, blasting music she'd written and recorded, burning V-8 rubber. While she tapped her foot on the gas pedal in time with the music, I'd touch up my makeup, jot lyrics to songs, and join her singing full voiced to Mary Chapin Carpenter's "Passionate Kisses." I was happy to be the Thelma to her Louise.

We became regular fixtures in the front row of Marianne Williamson's weekly lectures. With hands under our chins and stars in our eyes, we were true-blue Course in Miracles devotees. One night, as we hung on to Marianne's every syllable like it was gold (because it was), Gypsy leaned over and whispered, "Wouldn't it be great if we could be her opening act?" I thought, *Yeah . . . right.*

A few months later, Gypsy and I were Marianne Williamson's opening act, singing songs we'd written, warming up her audience. Nothing could get in Gypsy's way once her determination took hold. During a Sunday service at Agape, while Reverend Michael Beckwith was rattling the rafters with his heavenly infused message, Gypsy turned to me and whispered, "Wouldn't it be great to be Reverend Michael's opening act?" Before I could blink, Gypsy and I were onstage at Agape, singing our songs, warming up the audience for Reverend Michael.

Gypsy's next bright idea was recording our songs in legitimate studios, followed by a professional photo shoot with the help of our own personal glam squad: our friend Nicole coifed our hair, Stacy contoured our makeup, Eirylis choreographed our moves, Gina styled our wardrobe, Vivian became our manager, and Josh grabbed his camera and started snapping our photos. We were becoming ready for the big time . . . at least in our minds.

After many thoughtful conversations, we decided to name our singing group Zuzu's Petals, as a nod to Jimmy Stewart's portrayal of George Bailey in *It's a Wonderful Life*. In the movie, George Bailey discovered his daughter's (Zuzu's) wilted rose petals in his pocket at the moment he realized he was granted a second chance at life. With his aha moment literally in hand, instead of seeing his life through the lens of shattered dreams and dashed hopes, he realized his life was wonderful (thus the movie's title).

The name of our band was symbolic of the wake-up call Gypsy and I were constantly courting, trying to access in our lives, in our friendships, and in the lyrics of our songs.

Gypsy's next brilliant plan was to show up at a party that a particularly talented film director was rumored to be attending. Her plan was to inspire him to make us a music video. She met and inspired him so much that he, soon thereafter, proposed marriage. Our music video never materialized, but after a quick trip to city hall and practically before the ink could dry on their marriage certificate, Gypsy was pregnant. Then a few months after her daughter was born, she became pregnant with another baby girl.

The marriage didn't last long, but Gypsy's daughters became the center of her heart and soul and the beginning and end of her every breath and thought. She was fiercer than a pack of momma lions and was determined to do anything and everything to give her daughters whatever they needed to thrive. This was not easy to do, since she lived on the fringes of Malibu where the bar was set sky-high, as nearly all the girls' friends were children of the rich, famous, and infamous—and Gypsy was a single, working-her-ass-off mom. But in true Gypsy spirit, she pulled off the impossible every day and became a one-woman miracle-manifesting machine. Around Gypsy's juggling and struggling, she called me for prayer. Together we contacted God more often and feverishly than the Pope and the Dalai Lama combined.

Even though our big music plans became third fiddle to her daughters, our friendship never wavered. We talked on the phone or saw each other nearly every day, through ups and downs and multiple marriages (did I mention she was a hopeful romantic, our resident Elizabeth Taylor?). Besides calling ourselves Thelma and Louise, we were also like Emma Thompson and Kate Winslet in *Sense and Sensibility*. Gypsy was Kate (sense), always taking the wild leap for love. I was Emma (sensibility), erring on the side of rationality. Even though those who know me would never in a billion years accuse me of being rational, in our relationship, Gypsy was the kite, and I was on the ground, holding the string, watching her fly.

Speaking of flight, Gypsy budgeted all year every year so she could afford to fly annually to her beloved Italy. Her fourth husband was from Italy. Of course she loved him, but marrying him, though for only a short and sweet while, was (from my perspective) more about her making official her love affair with Italy. She was madly in love with the people, the men, the food, the men, the wine, the men, the way of life that appreciates and pedestalizes beauty, the men, art and song, and, oh yes, let's not leave out the men.

I received the blessing of being there with her once for a very short time. I regret it couldn't have been longer and more often. My first glance of Gypsy and Italy was after she had been flying all night on a red-eye. Most people would be exhausted and needing a day to sleep before coming out to play, but she and her bright-blue eyes were on full sparkle mode, so full of exploding joy.

Then just after Valentine's Day, 2018, I got a call from Gypsy, squealing with excitement about the fact that she'd reconnected with Gregory, a man she'd been friends with years before. She was certain he was "the one." I could tell she was determined, and I knew better than to dampen her excitement with my grounded sensibility—besides, I felt the trueness of their connection.

I had the honor of marrying Gypsy and Gregory twice—once in my living room right after she'd been diagnosed with cancer, so Gregory would be able to be with her during her treatments at the hospital. The second time I was honored to marry them was on the most magical day in Jenner by the Sea. In Gregory she found a devoted partner, and even though they'd only been romantically connected for a short time, he was her hero during the roughest time in Gypsy's life.

The hardest thing for me was when Gypsy would say, "Kell Bell, promise me I'm going to be OK." I'd tell her, "If anybody can beat this, it would be you."

I won't sugarcoat it. The last months of Gypsy's life were brutal. But ever-resilient Gypsy left sparks of beauty and joy everywhere she went. Even as she battled cancer, her makeup bag was never far behind. A month before her final days, I was at her home. "Sweet Love," the Stevie Nicks and Kenny Loggins song, played on the radio, and with the first notes of the song, even though she'd been in excruciating pain, Gypsy dropped her icepacks and popped off the couch and danced with me in the living room—a room never more appropriately named.

I think if it wasn't for how much she loved her daughters and husband, Gregory, she probably would have exited the planet sooner than she did. Instead, she held on, always with hope. Just like the title of her last album, *There's Still Hope*. As long as she was alive, she and all of us were hopeful, right until the bitter end.

But even the most determined, sensual, brilliant poets and fighters all have an expiration date. When she passed, she was surrounded by family and friends in her home in Jenner by the Sea—where, as Van Morrison sang, she sailed "Into the Mystic . . ."

Here's how I OGLE'd it:

O: *What is the Offending behavior and/or situation?*

Gypsy got cancer and died an excruciatingly painful death—and left behind people (including children and a husband and ex-husbands) who depended on her in a million intertwined ways. I'll miss her forever and will always feel she died too soon.

Cancer took from her so many of the aspects of life she loved—her ability to sing, kiss, eat, drink wine, and smoke (politically incorrect as that may be). And then after the surgeon carved the cancer from her tongue, to rebuild a new one, he moved a vein and a skin graft from her left wrist—taking from her, or so we thought, her decades-present whale and dolphin tattoos.

G: *What is Good about that offending behavior and/or situation?*

I could be upset at cancer for taking Gypsy away from me, ripping me off—but I could also simply be grateful for the time I did get with her. I also thank Hillary (Gypsy's first daughter, with whom she's now reunited) for bringing Gypsy to me.

Gypsy lived a rich and full life. She loved with her whole heart as much and as often as she could. Dannion Brinkley, a frequent flier to the other side (he's died four times), told Gypsy during a session, "Don't think of your cancer as your failure. See it as you've fulfilled your covenant. You came here to do what you came here to do, and now you are complete. As a reward for having done a great job, you get to go home. And when you get there, you will be comforted, grateful, filled with relief, and everything will make sense."

L: *How am I peering into the Looking Glass (mirror)?*

A part of me died when Gypsy left. We had so many plans—I was attached to her like she was attached to her husband and daughters.

Even though smoking was the likely culprit for Gypsy's cancer, I can't help but think it was also related to her biting her tongue as often as she did. In the spirit of wanting harmony in her life and wanting everyone to get along, she reined in the darker feelings on her palate. In service to harmony, in the past, I've also repressed my darker, shadowier feelings. But no more.

E: *How will I allow this situation to Elevate me? What Elevated action will I take?*

I believe nature never takes something away from you without giving you something in return.

After removing Gypsy's dolphin and whale tattoos from her wrist, the surgeon grafted them onto her tongue.

I joked with her and said, "Now you speak whale." She smiled and seemed to like that.

Back home, a couple of days after Gypsy passed, as I earlier mentioned, I pulled a card from my *Hero's Journey Dream Oracle Deck* and demanded: "Gypsy, where are you, and what are you doing?"

Here's the card I pulled, and what it said in full:

WHALE OF A TIME

Own your largess

Most people think of the belly of the whale stage of the hero's journey as a dark night of the soul, but it doesn't have to be … You have the ability to go with the flow, and the potential to own your power. When you contemplate the nature of this loving, ancient being we call whale—envision swimming with it and receiving its wisdom and love—you are reminded that you are sovereign, wild, and free. The whale is here to remind you whenever you find yourself in a challenging circumstance, your charge is to enlarge. Your mandate is to become a heart space so large the world can fit within it. . . . This card is your reminder to stop resisting, and instead, open and allow the diversity of life and the entire ocean of emotion of all sentient beings to be celebrated and loved.

Mantra: As I embrace my inner whale, my heart grows as big and deep as the ocean.[39]

I now think of Gypsy every time I see or hear mention of whales, dolphins, sea creatures, or mermaids. I've made it my mission to avoid the seduction of morbid grief by looking for signs of Gypsy. When I look, I find them everywhere. I believe when we tune in to the frequency of our loved ones on the other side, there is no vacuum. Even in our sorrow, we can ask them for a sign, and when we get it, we can revel in it, savor its flavor it like a full-bodied chianti, and swim in the deep end of their supernatural presence that remains, on a parallel plane, forever.

My Ass
Is on the Line

Southern California

*It is no measure of health to be well adjusted
to a profoundly sick society.*

—KRISHNAMURTI

I dreamed I was winning an award, on a public stage, à la the
Academy Awards. The award was for Best People Pleaser. Instead
of receiving a golden statue, my award was a bejeweled dress. I was
told by the director to change into it onstage, in front of everyone.
I argued, "Can't I go backstage to a changing room?" But she was
firm: "No."

Even though I resisted, award-winning people pleaser that I was,
I did what I was told. Modest, and a touch rebellious, I turned my
back and tried to quickly wriggle into the dress before the audience
could see too much of my backside. But much to my horror, the

dress was too tight, and the zipper got stuck . . . beneath my bare derriere!

I woke up with a start, disturbed and unable to shake the feeling of shame and "em-bare-ass-ment." As the day shuffled on, the dread from my dream haunted me, so I OGLE'd it.

O: *What is the Offending behavior and/or situation?*

This dream was so horrible and shocking . . . not a bloody, gutsy kind of nightmare, but a nightmare nonetheless.

This dream brought to the surface that which I'd successfully been able to ignore for a long time: I'd been a massive people pleaser, wanting external approval, positive feedback, and validation that stemmed from a fickle sense of inner invalidation. Yuck!

G: *What is Good about that offending behavior and/or situation?*

My lifelong question has always been "How can I be fully me while not rocking the boat so hard it flips over?" But sometimes the boat just needs to tip. We all have survival strate-gies for coping with this crazy world. People pleasing, knowing how to make others happy, knowing how to read a room and figure out what it will take to put a smile on people's faces is not the worst kind of survival strategy. It worked. I've survived. I'm still alive.

I thank God for the dream that let me become aware I have behav-iors with an expiration date that are ready to leave in a blaze of glory.

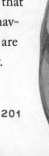

L: *How am I peering into the Looking Glass (mirror)?*

I believe every dream is a mirror of what's alive inside of us. My mom told me that when I was young, I was always asking to know what the rules were. That didn't mean I didn't break them. I was a sneaky sort of rebel who got her need for self-expression met behind the scenes.

In my dream, I'm not just the woman receiving the award but I'm also the director. That means I am the one behind the scenes orchestrating the whole production. In other words, I have more control over my circumstances than I realized. I agreed to the rules. And now I can change the rules, should I choose.

E: *How will I allow this situation to Elevate me? What Elevated action will I take?*

Because this dream rattled me to my core, I had to remind myself what I preach to my clients and students: "There's no such thing as a bad dream because a nightmare is an unfinished dream. The dream isn't over until you've redirected it to an empowered conclusion. So, how will you finish your dream?"

With this in my mind, I reentered the dream, from an awake, meditative state, and attempted to finish it . . . but I still couldn't shake the sickening feeling. If I've learned nothing else in my twenty-five-plus years of dreamwork, it's when all else fails, get creative. So, I went deep, with a pickax and shovel, excavated what was beneath this dream, and came through it with this poem, affectionately titled . . .

No Ifs, Ands, or BUTTs
My ass is hanging out onstage tonight
in front of everyone;
my worst fear expressed

because I can't fit in my dress.
I'm supposed to be receiving an award
a reward for being a people pleaser extraordinaire
Like Fred Astaire, on air
Minus Ginger Rogers
'cause she's not there.
She's trying so hard to get it right
holding tight
to the rope she walks.
Trying hard to do what she's been told,
trying hard to not grow old
trying hard to not be too bold
'Cause they won't like you, won't love you
won't protect you, won't accept you, won't respect you
In fact, they'll reject you.
But what the BLEEP!
I did what they said.
I became the walking dead.
I wore the pretty dress
they swore would look best
on me and my figure.
Now they'll have an image that's sure to linger
of me in my naked glory
wriggling into their ridiculous story,
real quick before they can get a good look at my ass;
before they have time to ask,
"Why not use a changing room
or go backstage to a private womb?"
Because there is no backstage,
not at this age!
It's all up front, and there's nowhere to hide,
so you're forced to see my backside.

And the moon, she's full tonight.
I'm stuck in a dress that doesn't fit.
I'm stuck in my shame, and it feels like . . .
my people pleasing is broken.
That's it!
I quit.
I'm out.
I'm done.
Whoever you are!
See my white flag?
You've won!
I rip off the dress,
unzip my distress.
Leave the scene of the crime just in time,
naked as a jaybird walking a fine line.
I shake it all off, and then it hits me:
the worst thing happened,
my public humiliation,
my ass hanging out for all to see,
but I'm not dead; it didn't kill me.
I'm still me, in fact more me
'cause now I have permission to be,
surprised to be free
of the shackles that used to bind
me to the disease to please that made me blind
to the fact that I was in a Stepford trance.
But now I can do my own dance
to my own rhythm, and my own grooves,
to my own gyrations, and my own moves.
I could end this dream here and I'd be fine,
but my stage of shame is still behind.
I've got to go back and claim what's mine.

After all, it's my ass that's on the line.
I've got to figure out how to make it right,
how to plug into my light,
because how can I love if I'm not there?
How can I contribute if I don't care?
I have to participate, to integrate, to excavate, to retaliate,
at least put in my two cents.
Otherwise, it's not worth me wearing such a beautiful dress.
I deserve an award.
A reward for getting my ass back in my body,
for honoring my soul
that's worth more than gold.
In my acceptance speech, I'll share
about my glorious derriere
out there for all to see.
And it didn't kill me.
I'm still alive;
in fact, now I thrive.

After writing this poem, I took myself to the Hollywood Walk of Fame and purchased a nine-dollar gold Academy Award statuette from a souvenir shop. I presented the award to myself to honor me for having come a long way, baby, and for being the authentic, wild, version of myself I am today. After all, isn't this who I incarnated to be? In fact, I believe this is why we all came to this planet—to at first be what other people need us to be until we learn we can love people more, deeper, better when we are true to ourselves.

Oh yes, to take the "E" for Elevate to the next level, I have to tell you about what happened after I presented my doctoral dissertation, which was an overview of this book, including sharing my

OGLE formula. One of my classmates pointed out something that should've been obvious to me, but I'd missed it. In my younger years, I was the victim of other people (mostly men's) ogling, but now I've turned the tables and become the Ogler (with a capital 'O') and I'm empowering others to be Oglers too—albeit in a transformational context. I love it when life comes full circle like that!

The Right to Bite

Southern California

In a dog's life, some plaster would fall, some cushions
would open, some rugs would shred.
Like any relationship, this one had its costs. They were costs we
came to accept and balance against the joy and amusement
and protection and companionship he gave us.

JOHN GROGAN

It was love at first hug.

On a hot Sunday morning in Brentwood, California, at the Cinco de Meow dog-and-cat rescue event, Dana and I did a pinky swear, looking deep into each other's eyes, making a pact that no matter how adorable the dogs were, we would not be taking one home.

Being allergic to cats, I knew felines weren't an option for me. Dana and I both, in our lives before we met, had been suckers for dogs. But we were getting married in just six weeks at our home, which meant we'd have a house filled with family, friends, and out-of-town guests—not at all a calm environment for an acclimating new pet. There would be more than enough chaos to manage amid the variety of personalities in the three-ring circus that would soon be under our roof. As it was, I was doing everything I could not to be Bridezilla. I didn't need one more stick of dynamite on top of an already highly flammable pile of stress. So, no dogs allowed. At least not for a long while after our wedding.

But then, amid the blaring pet-inspired music and brightly colored banners, a fluffy, blond, husky mix with a medium snout—the Zsa Zsa Gábor of dogs—beelined toward me, then stood on her hind legs. She didn't put her feet on my stomach like most dogs who jump on people do. She wrapped her puffy paws around my waist in a perfect slow dance, while smiling up at me. Her bright-pink tongue hung out to the side, while her brown eyes sparkled and a red heart on her collar announced, "Adopt Me!"

How in God's name could I say no? The word seemed to form itself automatically; like breathing or blood flowing, I couldn't stop it. "OK," I acquiesced, without any arm twisting.

The love was instant and unconditional. She followed me without need for a leash across this sunny, outdoor carnival. When Dana spotted us walking toward him, my soon-to-be-husband vigorously shook his head and yelled, "No! Absolutely not."

"But she's so cute," I pleaded, "and she's a hugger."

Before he could protest, she wrapped her furry paws around his waist, sprinkling her magic dust on Dana as she'd done with me. Then Dana, too, became helpless, putty in her paws. On the drive home, Dana asked, "Do we even know the breed of our new dog?"

I parroted what the woman we purchased her from had said: "We're not exactly sure of the breed, since she's a rescue, but we think she's a husky-keeshond mix."

"What's her name?" Dana asked.

"They said her name is Satira, but that doesn't feel right. Let's dream on what she wants to be called."

Our new dog's first few days with us at Wedding Central was a bustling time. She curled up in a ball of fluff, nonplussed as she listened to Dana and I field nonstop phone calls from bridesmaids, groomsmen, friends, and family about directions, photographers, last-minute invitations and wedding decorations, parking permits, musicians, catering, and entertainment.

A few days later, I dreamed that our sweet new dog was in a criminal lineup, first straight on, then both profiles. She was wearing a red bandana around her neck and sporting a pistol in each of her front paws/hands, and the name scrawled beneath the Wanted Poster read, "Woofero Wooferino: AKA Woofie Dog."

I woke up with a start, pushing away any notion that this could be foreboding, as I yelled out, "Woofie!" She came right to me, wagging her tail. When I told Dana about the dream, I said my interpretation was, "Woofie must've felt so awful having been abandoned, and it's up to us to let her know how totally *wanted* she is."

After a week, as the shock of being in a new environment wore off and the tranquilizing effect of the drugs the adoption agency must've given her began to wane, Woofie's true colors began to peek out beneath her mellow façade. I found wedding gift packages torn asunder, end tables with chew marks, pillows and cushions with upholstery torn to bits. Our previously chillaxed dog couldn't stop running in circles around the house, scampering under our feet, and snarling at anyone who got close to her, excluding Dana and me. On top of that, the neighbors complained that whenever Dana and I left her alone she'd howl in such a mournful, sorrowful way that it upset the whole block.

What had we gotten ourselves into?

At three o'clock on June 29, 2002, Pachelbel's Canon in D played through the speakers, followed by our friend singing Shania Twain's "You're Still the One." I walked down the rose-petalled aisle in my long, white, lace gown toward a radiantly handsome, smiling Dana standing proudly in his kaftan. Surrounded by loved ones and a bevy of my friends (aka the goddesses), amid the scent of earthy sage and sweet embers of palo santo, Dana and I spoke our vows. Our three shaman ministers (yes, we felt the need to have three to shepherd us through this epic rite of passage) pronounced us husband and wife. Just then, Woofie made a prison break from her locked tower (aka our upstairs bedroom), sending shockwaves throughout the congregation.

Just like in a scene from *Marly and Me*, the movie about a loveable but destructive dog, Woofie knocked down everything in her wake. Like a heat-seeking missile, she flew across the aisle, sending rose petals in to the air, and then planted herself between Dana and me, just in time for the kiss.

I did my best to quell the pandemonium by grabbing the microphone and announcing, "Our new dog wanted to be included in our vows. No one puts Woofie in the corner."

The crowd roared, and we kissed, but when the minister tried to move her, she snapped at him, so we let her remain with us for the benediction.

At the reception, one of Dana's groomsmen fastened his boutonniere on Woofie's collar. I surrendered to letting her join the reception—luckily, without a hitch. After one of my friends punched my second cousin in the nose for making a sexist remark, Woofie became the second-most-talked-about highlight of our wedding.

Following the wedding, I learned the hard way not to let Woofie walk the canyon unleashed. She'd walk by most dogs wagging her tail; then out of nowhere, she'd lunge into attack mode. Woofie's antics crescendoed the day our friend puckered her lips and went in for a kiss. She ignored Woofie's warning growls and my pleading, and Woofie bit her. Our friend's lip was punctured (and so was her pride); she was OK, but I was hysterical.

As hard as I tried to normalize the Woofie situation, I could not prevent the horrible night my friend Natasha came over to our house for a birthday celebration. As the festivities wound down, her young son, Brandon, played in the driveway. Out of nowhere, Woofie leaped at him, biting him on the belly. The night ended with Natasha and Brandon in the hospital and Dana and me having a heartbreaking conversation. Dana said through tears, "We have to put Woofie down. She's a liability, a danger, and a threat."

This shattered my heart, even though I knew it was true. I tossed and turned all night and woke up the next morning crystal clear— I could not put her down. I became resolute I would no longer make light of Woofie's behavior. It was my job as her adopted caretaker to take care of her, to fix her, and to take the problem into my own hands.

It was time to call in the big guns. Dana and his friend Skip had a pet business (literally), Laurel Canyon Animal Company, making music for animals, and had become friendly with a corral of animal psychics.[40] One of them did a session with Woofie. This entailed her sitting next to our dog in silence for about twenty minutes and scratching notes on a pad of paper, nodding at the inaudible words Woofie was supposedly speaking to her.

Ultimately, the pet psychic told us in a hushed tone, "As a wee pup, Woofie was abused and mistreated and left to fend for herself.

She's triggered by loud groups and does not want anyone, animal or human, near her face. She loves being your dog, and she takes her role as your protector, very seriously. Oh yes, she's deathly afraid you will one day leave her, as her other caretakers have. This may be the cause of her anxiety."

"I would never leave her," I quickly replied.

"Then I suggest telling her so, every day."

"OK, I will. Then will she stop biting people?"

The psychic looked at Woofie, who was fastidiously licking her feet, not appearing to me to be saying anything at all except, *Hey, check out my clean feet.*

But a few minutes later, with a downcast look, the psychic admitted, "No matter how strong of a case I try to make with her, Woofie refuses to give up her right to bite."

Soon after the session with the psychic, I met with a dog shaman, and a trainer, then another trainer touted for being able to tame the most vicious dogs. But after all that, Woofie still had a wild streak. So, I took it on myself, for the following ten years, to keep her on a very, very short leash. I made grand disclaimers to anyone who dared come to our house and to the people we passed on the trail: "Sorry, my dog is extremely protective . . . she might bite if you get too close."

To this, neighbors either recoiled in terror upon seeing her or they'd laugh, watching Woofie nearly pull my arm out of its socket, yelling out, "Who's walking who?"

When she passed away (of natural causes) on Valentine's Day 2013, at the age of fourteen (seventy-eight in human years), she hadn't attacked any other beings, human or canine, for her remaining ten years.

As we buried her skinny yet still fluffy body in our backyard, I howled nonstop like a member of a pack of heartbroken wolves, crying harder than I'd ever cried before. I'd never felt the ache of losing a being I was attached to more than her.

Here's how I OGLE'd it:

O: *What is the Offending behavior and/or situation?*

Woofie's aggressive, protective, erratic way was so stressful. The fact that she could be so loving and tender in one moment, then unpredictably ferocious the next made me feel like I was in an abusive relationship—in love and devoted to a soul so sweet, loving, and caring . . . who could flip from Dr. Jekyll to Mr. Hyde at a moment's notice.

G: *What is Good about that offending behavior and/or situation?*

According to the pet psychic, Woofie's aggression must have saved her life during a time when it was truly threatened. She also considered Dana and me part of her pack. Her misguided, trigger-happy defenses were meant to keep us all safe.

Oh yes, we live in an area where coyotes are the terrors of the neighborhood. During Woofie's reign, I didn't fear the coyotes one bit—in fact, she was their biggest nightmare.

One good thing came from the horrific drama of Woofie biting Natasha's son, Brandon. The next day at school, Brandon did a show-and-tell, revealing his bandages, and soon became the coolest kid in kindergarten. Years later, as a young adult, he shared with me that his scar became a badge of honor that won him serious "street cred" all the way through high school.

L: *How am I peering into the Looking Glass (mirror)?*

In the same way the psychic said Woofie was trigger-happy because of her past traumas, I can also pre-react and be overly quick to defend myself or those I love. I can see how my overzealous, adrenalized intensity has a power and volition of its own—and by reacting, the pain I cause others and myself can be tragic in that it snuffs out the joy, connection, and intimacy that can only happen in a space of emotional safety.

E: *How will I allow this situation to Elevate me? What Elevated action will I take?*

As Caroline Myss says, the purpose of our lives is to manage our power—even though most of us, myself included, often don't realize we have any power worth managing.[41] The truth is we do, I do, and that power can be used to enhance or detract from the people around us. These days, I like to imagine I'm a black belt in karate (even though, in reality, the highest belt I ever achieved in tae kwon do was blue). I don't need to show off how powerful I am. My knowing transmits as a preventative force field, curtailing real or imagined threats to my well-being.

A month after Woofie crossed the rainbow bridge, I was walking along the boardwalk in Venice Beach, and out of the corner of my eye, I saw a dog who looked exactly like her at her prime. The dog had the same fluffy hair, medium snout, brown eyes, and red tongue. Never before had I seen another dog who was her exact replica.

My heart leaped out of my body, tears stung my eyes, and I ran over to Woofie's twin. I approached the man holding the leash, who cautioned in an eerily familiar way, "Sorry, she's extremely protective . . . she might bite if you get too close."

Since Woofie had been a rescue, her veterinarian and I guessed her to be a husky mix, but were never crystal clear, so I asked the man, "What kind of dog is she?"

He guffawed. "She not a dog. She's an Alaskan wolf."

I stood in shock, remembering the dream I had about her in the wanted poster revealing her name, which now made perfect sense:

Holy God! All this time, Woofie wasn't a bad dog. She was a good wolf!

Maybe we're all more powerful than we believe ourselves to be, wolves in dog clothing, comparing ourselves to unattainable Stepfordian standards that were never ours to begin with. Maybe we'd be better off just being the best wolves we can be, maintaining our wildness, while howling our grief, longing, and passion to the full moon. And while milling through domesticated polite society, let's relinquish our right to bite . . . unless absolutely necessary.

Diamond in the Mud

Whittier, CA

There is the mud, and there is the lotus that grows out of the mud. We need the mud in order to make the lotus.

THICH NHAT HANH

Like a criminal before the gallows, head hanging low, frozen with fright, I peered up through my lashes at my dad, who was a ball of fury as he shook my red-marked paper. I was nine years old, and we sat on the edge of our living room couch in terrible silence for what felt like an hour, except for the sound of my sniffles and his rattling of the paper.

My dad was a quintessential alpha male, a born leader, which led to him being the chief of police in one of the toughest crime districts in Los Angeles. He'd been a boxer, a weightlifter, and a runner. He'd never admit it, but I imagined he'd wanted sons, but all he got were daughters, five of them. So, as the eldest of his daughters, as I grew up, he was my coach for soccer, softball, and track. He'd cheer me on from the sidelines to run faster, lift my knees higher, kick the ball harder, and shake off the pain faster when I'd get whacked in the shins.

After the game, no matter how poorly I played, he'd give me an enveloping hug, followed by his sparkling eyes imploring me along, "Who loves you?"

I'd respond sheepishly, "You, Dad."

"You got that right," he'd beam with a squeeze.

The glow of his validation—even when undeserved—calmed my jitters and gave me the sense that all was right with the world . . . or at least it would be.

I was grateful he abdicated everyday front-line duty to my mom when it came to dealing with my sisters and me. Chief Sullivan would jump to high alert for life-and-death matters. But on a day-to-day basis, he was too caught up in running the police department to worry about which of his daughters needed tampons, acne cream, or a shoulder to cry on due to boyfriend drama.

As a kid, I dreaded his dark mood that would sometimes follow him home from the police station like a malevolent hitchhiker. After all, he was dealing with the dregs of society all day: drug dealers, murderers, and rapists. When his sunny skies turned stormy, my world unhinged, which must've accounted, at least in large part, for why I become such a people pleaser. To make him smile, I'd perform my latest cheerleading routine, dazzling the troops (him and my family) with fan kicks and pom-pom tosses in the air, catching them behind my back with a twirl punctuated by dropping into the splits.

But there were times when all my best jazzy moves couldn't lift his spirit. Like when my uptight, bespectacled fourth-grade teacher, Mrs. Bickford, gave the class a word-search puzzle. I thought it was hilarious when I found and circled four-letter cuss words. Mrs. Bickford didn't find it one bit charming. In fact, she was so perturbed by my "disrespectful conduct," she called a parent-teacher conference to discuss my offenses. When my mom and dad came home from that dreaded meeting, my dad's voice shook the house as he bellowed my name.

I sat shivering beside him on the couch. He finally broke the angry silence with "God dammit! I know you learned those words from me. It's not right to tell you to do what I say, not what I do . . . but that's exactly what I'm telling you to do." Then he surprised me with "Kelly, you are a diamond—beautiful, precious. When you use words like . . . these"—he lifted the foul paper as his voice cracked—"it's like dropping a diamond into mud. Don't do that. It breaks my heart."

I lifted my gaze from the floor to his teary, sapphire eyes, jumped up, and wrapped my arms around his neck. "I'm sorry, Dad."

Here's how I (eventually) OGLE'd it:

O: *What is the Offending behavior and/or situation?*

Mrs. Bickford ratted me out—caught me doing something naughty—and shamed me by calling my parents. My dad scared me—I hated his dark moods that made me feel unsafe and instilled in me the disease to please.

G: *What is Good about that offending behavior and/or situation?*

Mrs. Bickford was just doing her job. If I'd been in her (sensible) shoes, I might've done the same. It's good to be called out on my potty mouth (or mind) so that when I do choose to cuss, I make it count.

Oh yes, Mrs. Bickford set the stage for one of my favorite memories of my dad—that I wouldn't trade for all the cuss words in the world.

L: *How am I peering into the Looking Glass (mirror)?*

I am now the critic of my life, making red marks all over the places where I misstep and misspeak. As a grown-up (for a while now), I'm sure I don't know how scary I can be to the people around me when I get angry.

E: *How will I allow this situation to Elevate me? What Elevated action will I take?*

I think of this moment often, and it melts my heart. What stands out to me the most was my dad's willingness to be vulnerable and honest about his shortcomings. Yes, he could be scary, but his heart was pure gold, and he demonstrated a brilliant parenting technique: instead of telling me I was wrong, broken, and bad for what I'd done, he told me how precious I was—and showed me the high bar he'd set for me. He was disappointed in my behavior because he expected more of me.

I'd like to say I never dropped an f-bomb after that incident in fourth grade, but I'd be effing lying. But because of this incident, I'm more mindful of the words I speak than I might otherwise have been. And I know, beyond a shadow of a doubt, no matter how many mud puddles I've fallen into over the course of my life, they don't define me. Besides, if my dad sees me as a diamond, I must not be all bad.

Kelly versus the Volcano

Guatemala

Do not go gentle into that good night,
Old age should burn and rave at close of day;
Rage, rage against the dying of the light.

DYLAN THOMAS

The elevation was so high, I could only crawl one or two steps at a time. Exhaustion crept in, and I had to stop and catch my breath. Crouched on a rock, I heard slippery pebbles cascade down around me. I shakingly sipped my nearly empty bottle of water and nibbled a ration of my remaining Clif bar. Like a robot, I did my best to mute the voice of panic yelling, *You shouldn't have done this. You ignored the queasy feeling in your belly, and now, because of your stupid ego, this is how you'll die.*

In an attempt to make sense of how I got there, hanging off the edge of a volcano by clutching branches and roots, I mentally replayed the events of the previous few months . . .

It was five months before my fiftieth birthday, and I was feeling an existential compulsion to do something radical. I puzzled over what stunt I could pull that would turn back the hands of time, or at least show myself I wasn't done with life and life wasn't done with me.

I was delighted when my husband and I met successful corporate CEO, bestselling author of *The High Performance Life*, philanthropist, and extreme athlete Joe Gagnon. He shared with us that he was always looking for opportunities to explore the edge of his physical capacities. Inspired, the three of us brain-/heart-stormed about what he/we could do to raise awareness and money for underprivileged kids in Guatemala, where our nonprofit program had been focused.

We learned there were thirty-seven Guatemalan volcanos, and of those, seven were perfect for climbing. Since the year before Joe had completed the Six Continent Challenge (he ran a marathon on six different continents in six consecutive days), we decided he should do what we now called Seven Volcano Challenge. In this new test of his strength and fortitude, Joe and a group of athletes would summit a volcano a day for seven consecutive days.

My job was in a supportive role, as the liaison to the media and the organizations our efforts were benefiting and to make sure all went smoothly. To rally excitement and additional donations among the people in my social media sphere, I pledged I would climb at least one volcano. Never having climbed a volcano, I had no idea what it entailed, but when I ran cross-country in high school, I used to summit hills all the time. How hard could it be?

The day came, and our lively bunch met at the foot of the first volcano, Tacaná, the second-highest peak in Central America at 13,320 feet, in the Sierra Madre de Chiapas of northern Guatemala. Bustling with our crew, media, and teenagers from our program, the scene was festive. With our well-wishes, we sent Joe, the guides, and the young people off.

Once the joy of our pep rally concluded, I felt like confetti littering the ground in Times Square after the New Year's ball had dropped. Even though I loved being in the midst of this exciting altruistic venture, I hated to admit feeling a tinge of FOMO. While everyone else was doing all the death-defying fun stuff, I felt like the little old lady left behind, safe and secure but missing out on the sidelines.

That night at dinner, while the group regaled us with tales of their exciting quest, over the ruckus, my ears perked when I thought I heard someone mention the next volcano would be the smallest and easiest to climb. *If ever there was going to be a volcano for me, this would be it.*

With this in mind, the next day I shoehorned myself into the group, which consisted of Joe, the guides, the kids, and the mother of two of the teenagers. Apparently Adventurous Mom also thought she was too young to be a Sideline Granny.

On this warm but cloudy day, we arrived at the second volcano, Tajumulco. The kids and Joe shot out of the van like rockets, while Adventurous Mom and I followed behind at a slower pace. About a half an hour up a winding but gentle path, we arrived at a shady spot with a beautiful overlook. Adventurous Mom removed her backpack and declared, "This is it for me."

I was still full of energy and determination to make it to the top, since this was the smallest volcano of them all and probably my one shot to summit. I asked, "Would you be OK if I go ahead and try to make it to the top?"

She nodded with a warm smile. "Of course."

"I imagine I shouldn't be gone for more than thirty to sixty minutes."

She said she'd be fine as she opened her knapsack beneath a generous tree, removing her snacks and water. With her diary in hand, she reassured me, "This is a perfect place to write in my journal and maybe do some yoga. I've been craving some alone time. It's fine. I'll be here when you come down."

I double- and triple-checked to make sure she was OK to be left alone, and she said a hearty yes every time. So, I bid her adieu and jogged along the path the others had blazed just a few minutes before. In spite of the queasy feeling in my belly and reprimanding voice in my head shouting, *This is a bad idea*, my ego was determined to prove fifty was the new thirty. When else would I ever get the chance to demonstrate I had the spunk to summit a volcano?

I continued meandering along the path until one of the guides yelled to me from way ahead, "No hay camino!" (There is no path!) I could see what he was talking about; the path suddenly bumped against a steep incline covered in juniper trees, red pine, and sage bushes. It was a cloudy day, and I couldn't see the top of the volcano from where I was. I assumed that, like Joe and the group, I'd have to forge my own path up the steep incline, arguing with the dull ache in my gut. *Come on! How hard can it be to make it to the top of this teensy-weensy volcano? It's just a glorified hill.*

However, as I ascended, the fog became denser and denser, making it impossible to see more than a few feet ahead at a time. I told myself, *I must be getting close. Just keep going, straight up until you reach the top. This is the bunny slope compared to the black diamonds. Any second, I'll be there.*

But the harder and farther I scaled, the shorter of breath and sleepier and more nauseous I became. The grade had become nearly vertical, and the only way to advance along the incline was to grip the branches, twigs, and roots jutting out of the side of the volcano.

The high elevation made me feel like a ninety-year-old, only able to crawl one or two steps at a time. I crouched above a rock with pebbles falling down around me. I tried to distract myself from hearing the voice of panic yelling, *Because of your ego, this is how you'll die.*

I took my next weary step on what looked like a rock but slipped as the rock turned to powdered ash and bounced its way down the canyon. I shakingly gripped the rough, prickly juniper branches to hoist me another few feet.

Keep going. At any minute, you'll hit the top and all will be well. To turn around now, five minutes before the miracle, would defeat the purpose of all my effort.

I pulled out my phone in hopes of getting one tiny dot of service on this remote spot to call the group and let them know where I was. Just as I noticed the time, the phone's sputtering battery gasped its last breath. I'd been gone over an hour and a half, way longer than I'd told Adventurous Mom, and I still wasn't at the top—and had no idea how much farther I had to go. A vision of the cheering reunion with the group once I made it gave me the energy to take my next step, and my next.

In the eerie quiet, I reviewed our dinner gathering the night before. I remembered Angel, the stocky guide seated next to me at the restaurant, saying something about how the ancient Mayan sacerdotes (priests) had the power to not only tame serpents but awaken the fury of the volcanos.

"Do they ever erupt when you're hiking?" I asked. "Do you get a warning? Might that happen on this trip?"

"The volcanos we'll mount on this journey have been inactive for a while," he replied thoughtfully, "but we can never guarantee how it will go. Sometimes the volcano gods give us a warning before they erupt—sending steam rising from the top, or an earthquake. But if the gods get angry, they can erupt at any time. We have to respect them."

I wish I'd paid more attention when he described the ways the ancient Mayans prayed and made offerings to seek the volcano gods' favor. I offered my own, more of a pleading than a prayer: *Please don't hurt me. Please let me find my group soon. Let us all survive this.*

Blinded by the mist, cursing myself for going against my gut feeling, I yelled out, "HELLO! CAN ANYONE HEAR ME?" I regretted not wearing something more colorful so I could be found. My gray T-shirt with black yoga pants made me blend in with the rocks. I stopped yelling, realizing I needed to ration my energy.

This was how the next hour went: take a step, stop, sit, catch my breath, sip water, clamber up a couple of steps, stop, rest, repeat. Until the triumphant moment finally arrived. I reached what must've been the top because the grade was, finally, gloriously, flat. But there was no group there to applaud my Herculean effort. And what made this moment even more anticlimactic was being surrounded by gray cotton-ball clouds. I couldn't look down and see the valley below and marvel at how high I'd climbed. I could barely see my hands stretched out in front of me. Despite being alone and having no vista as a reward for my effort, my entire body took a deep breath of relief, knowing I'd done it. I'd made it to the top of . . . something.

Surrounded in vapor, I hollered to see if my teammates were there. "HELLO!" I yelled out again, trying to pierce the sonic insulation of the cloud covering. "IS ANYONE HERE? IT'S KELLY! WHERE ARE YOU GUYS?"

I waited to hear the faintest response, but the haze muted my sound. All I could hear was the faint squawking of birds singing their secret language to each other. I was delirious enough to take it personally. I imagined them wondering who the gringa was infiltrating their nest.

Dizzy, I felt like I was the only person on the planet. This was not the celebratory experience I had imagined: looking down from a lofty perch, joining my comrades with hugs, high fives, and fist bumps. Where could they be?

I figured they were just obscured by the clouds and unable to hear me through them. I decided I'd better loop back and start the arduous hike down the pathless path. I'd already been gone way longer than I'd expected. I hoped no one was worried.

Then I heard a noise, a yell, the wonderous sound of a human. As the voice became louder, I could see it belonged to the guide I'd talked with the night before, Angel.

Relief washed over me like a cool rain in the parched desert. *I'm no longer alone. Help is here!*

In Spanish he asked what the hell I was doing. I responded, "Trying to follow the rest of the group . . . since this was the smallest volcano, I figured this was the one I should climb."

He looked at me like I'd just escaped from the loony bin. "No, honey, this is one of the biggest volcanos. You shouldn't be up here."

But, but . . . I replayed the snippet of conversation from the night before. Maybe my Spanish wasn't as good as I thought. Then he said, "The volcano we'll take on tomorrow will be the smallest one. But today, this is the biggest." Then he sweetly reprimanded me for climbing the wrong side. *Wrong side? What?*

I followed Angel around the volcano only to discover, "Hay camino!"—there was a path, beautiful and clear. It was just not where I had expected it to be.

Together, Angel and I walked down a most civilized path, not crawling like spiders the way I'd spent the last two hours—the way I would have done so going back down, had my guide not appeared to show me the way.

A measly half hour later, out of the cloud bank and into the sun, we arrived in the clearing where I'd left Adventurous Mom, who'd been reunited with our group.

So excited to see them, I ran ahead to give the long-awaited hugs, expecting to get pats on the back congratulating me for making it to the top. But they were wide-eyed with fury. They yelled, "What the hell were you thinking? That was so dangerous and selfish!" They reprimanded me for having left the other half of my "no grannies left behind" team alone and for stupidly venturing off by myself. Didn't I know the cardinal rule of volcano climbing? "Never go alone!"

No, I didn't know this rule since this was the first (and last) time I'd ever climb a volcano. The chastising continued, and I felt like a shamed puppy who'd just eaten someone's birthday cake.

The most heartbreaking part of this was that the kids who'd looked up to me, prior to my blunder, cast me off the pedestal I hadn't asked to be put on because I'd "abandoned" their mother. They felt devastated and betrayed. I asked Adventurous Mom how she was doing, since she'd seemed so content when I'd left her.

She averted her eyes and confessed, "I didn't want to be left alone. I was scared."

"What? Why did you say you were OK?"

"Because I knew that's what you wanted me to say."

Are you kidding me? I'm an award-winning people pleaser, but this is next level. I didn't know much about her, but I did know she was from a different culture than mine, and maybe that's where our miscommunication lay. I'd foolishly assumed she'd meant what she'd said.

By the grace of the volcano gods, despite my debacle, the Seven Volcano Challenge was a success, raising thousands of dollars in scholarships for impoverished young people. However, my relationships with the kids in my group were irreparably tainted. I may not have fallen into a volcano, but I did fall from grace, and it was devastating.

Here's how I OGLE'd it:

O: *What is the Offending behavior and/or situation?*

My heart was crushed at having let down the kids who, prior to this, had looked up to me. But I was also deeply hurt for being persecuted when I didn't mean any harm. I was let down that they didn't have more generosity, more room for me to be human, after all the arduous and painstaking blood, sweat, and years I'd poured into our nonprofit program. I didn't set out to maliciously hurt anyone. Besides, I never agreed to be their mom's babysitter.

However, as hurt as I was that they didn't give me a break, the most offensive behavior was my own. I was the one with the knot in my stomach when I left Adventurous Mom behind as I continued my quest. There was some part of me that knew I was out of alignment, but my ego was determined to prove I could climb that volcano. I was the one who picked the wrong moment to get my own needs met when my job was in a "giving" capacity. It was inappropriate for me to take something for myself, even if it seemed like an innocent enough souvenir/ early-birthday present.

G: *What is Good about that offending behavior and/or situation?*

No one can fall from grace unless they have been highly regarded. The kids and the rest of our group were so angry at me because they had projected perfection onto me, undeserved as it was.

I learned my intuition is keen and my will is powerful—and they're not always right. It's especially suspect when my ego gets involved.

Despite all the emotional pain I caused the group and myself, I had to admit, I did prove I had the stamina and perseverance to climb not just a pip-squeak of a volcano but what turns out to have been the highest peak in Central America, 13,845 feet. If that wasn't enough, I climbed the most grueling side. So, yes, I admit to a tiny bit of satisfaction knowing I was more athletic than I realized, not yet ready to claim AARP status.

Oh yes, the part of me that thought my actions didn't matter and didn't affect anybody can now be deleted from the record, Your Honor.

L: *How am I peering into the Looking Glass (mirror)?*

These kids threw me off the holier-than-thou pedestal, but nobody flicked me off harder than myself.

I'm also just like the kids who erroneously projected perfection onto me. I've done that to people who presented themselves in a leadership capacity, thinking they were so wonderful that I became crushed when they turned out to be fallibly human.

In fact, I felt just as devastated at the kids when they threw me into their inner volcano for my infraction. Leaders are human and deserve the generosity of tolerance when they make a mistake.

I'm firing myself from being anyone's role model. In some way I'd done the same thing with the kids, assuming they had a higher level of maturity than they did. Instead of being devasted, I could do to them what I wish they had done to me, which is take responsibility for my own projection.

Damn! As hard as it is to admit, I'm also just like Adventurous Mom—or at least, I used to be—saying and doing what I thought people wanted me to say and do. In my past, I didn't think I had the luxury of consulting my true feelings. Even though Adventurous Mom was from a different culture, where people say yes when they mean no because they're told it's more polite, it turns out she and I are not so different, after all.

But, like a volcano, what is suppressed must express. The times I said yes when I meant no eventually led to either an explosion or an implosion—neither of which are healthy. Spewing hot lava internally or externally blesses no one.

E: *How will I allow this situation to Elevate me? What Elevated action will I take?*

It's hard to take a more elevated action than climbing a volcano (ha ha), but out of this fiasco, here are the elevated insights I unpacked:

In the future, I'll do my best to keep my ego in check. There are safer ways to prove my vitality that won't put anyone at risk.

I've led enough sacred journeys with my pilgrimages to Teotihuacán, Mexico, to know we get the booby prize if nothing goes wrong. The moments when our plans fall apart become the moments of greatest learning and growing.

If I put someone on a pedestal they don't deserve to be on and they fall, I will take responsibility for my disappointment, instead of feeling entitled to rant and rave in victimhood.

If somebody should foolishly deify me, I'll hand them this book to read for themselves how fabulously flawed and fantastically fallible I am.

And if anyone demonizes me because I take the wrong path up the wrong side of the wrong volcano, I'll give myself the understanding and forgiveness I wish they'd give me.

A couple of months after we returned home, on June 3, 2018, one of the last volcanos Joe and the crew summitted, the 12,346-foot Fuego Volcano, erupted, killing 201 people, injuring 27, and leaving 260 people missing. The volcano emitted a five-mile stream of hot lava and a dense plume of black smoke and ash that blanketed Antigua, Guatemala's capital city, and other regions. I had no idea of the fire we were playing with on our Seven Volcano Challenge.

There's no perfect bow with which to wrap this story, other than to send prayers to the beautiful people of Guatemala. If there's any group of humans who know how to turn the tragic into magic, it's them. Guatamaltecos, as they call themselves, taught me so much more than simply beholding God in the volcanos. They taught me to tread with reverence not only for each other but for this sacred Mother Earth, whose bounty and body provide the home we're privileged to live in (and sometimes climb).

Conclusion

"Pain pushes until the vision pulls."
MICHAEL BECKWITH

As a dream therapist, I find most people don't feel moved to go to the trouble to book sessions with me when they're having a run of joyous dreams. It's the nightmares that are the biggest instigators of growth. It's those frightening dreams that are the fiery pokers that motivate people to jump through the rings of fire to seek me out. Because of this, I've been exposed to thousands of nightmares over the past twenty-five years. In fact, I've been given the title, in some circles, of the Nightmare Whisperer. I don't mind it one bit. In fact, I love it, because my ability to mine gold from even the most atrocious nightmares turns out to be my superpower.

Along those lines, I often get asked why we have so many nightmares. To that I reply, "They are the most commonly remembered dreams, but that's not because they're the most common dreams. Nightmares just happen to be the easiest ones to catch because they're so intense and emotionally dramatic. Like the saying goes, 'If it bleeds, it leads.'"

Difficult, painful, even tragic things will happen in our lives, no matter how high we build our castle walls, how many degrees we have, or how many likes we get on social media. It's not a matter of if, it's a matter of when, and what we're going to do when it does. In fact, it was in the contract we signed when we agreed to take a human incarnation. We were just so excited about the "get to have sex" part of being human, we skipped right past the caution in fine print.

The human part of me is sorry for any trauma or nightmares you've had to endure in this life (or any other). But the spiritual part of me knows there's a reason, and even if you can't identify it, you have the ability to use your experience for good.

For every one of our tragic moments, there are at least a thousand moments of magic that went unnoticed, perhaps because they were simply too subtle or we were in such a big hurry that we rushed right by them. As we evolve as a species, however, I believe that we will become more sensitive and, thus, receptive to the subtle, gentle blessings that rain down on us like freshly fallen snowflakes at all times, in our waking and in our sleeping dreams. When that ratio flips, and we live in such a state that we're more attuned to the magic than the tragic, I believe our work will be done.

Until then, I hope you'll carry the OGLE formula with you in your back pocket, making it your own, so you can transform into magic anything that resembles the tragic from a hundred paces. That way you can get back to the business of heightening your radar to perceive even the most vaporous blissful moments of magic happening all around you, at all times, even now.

Afterword

PERSEPHONE'S LAST WORD

Some scholars argue that Persephone might not have been as innocent as we thought. In fact, she might've been in cahoots with Hades all along, as she deliberately partook of the pomegranate seeds. Perhaps this was her unconscious attempt to accelerate her personal growth on behalf of all of us . . . turning the table, from being ogled to the Ogler.

Either way, I believe we should give thanks to (our inner) Persephone's tragic-to-magic journey. Thanks to her, we solved the age-old mystery about why good girls are drawn to bad boys, and according to myth, she gets credit for the four seasons we experience on earth instead of the monotony of nonstop springtime.

As you make transforming the tragic into magic your habit, you'll claim your place next to Persephone and me on the Mount Olympus of your own life, upon your throne, as a force to be reckoned with, as the unique healer/alchemist/bridge being you came here to be.

Acknowledgments

A book like this is impossible to do alone—not just the writing and the publishing but the living (and in some cases, the surviving) of it. It would be nearly—if not entirely—impossible to find the magic amid the tragic all by myself. The following earth angels, gods, and goddesses are people for whom I could write an entire book of praise. Please read between the lines to feel the depth of my gratitude that goes all the way to the center of the universe:

- Michele Ashtiani Cohn and Richard Cohn—thank you, Beyond Words, for your enthusiasm, guidance, and conscientious partnership. Thank you, Bailey Potter, for your attention to detail and compassionate heart. Lindsay Easterbrooks-Brown for making sure the manuscript was ready for showtime, and Brennah Hermo for her PR/ marketing savoir faire.

- My amazing agent, Devra Jacobs at Dancing Word Group (and Rebecca Stinson), for your belief in this book and in me. In a world of rough edges and closed doors, you have always been an open door (and heart) for me. My gratitude has no bounds!

- Dana Walden for winning the prize for most mentions in this book. I can't thank you enough for loving me and bearing with me through all of our life's many adventures over the past twenty-plus years (and twenty-plus lifetimes). For every one of our tragic moments, there have been innumerable magic moments that could fill volumes. Thank you for being the producer who wouldn't sleep with me, even though you have for more than two decades.

- Nancy T., for being my travel buddy throughout so many escapades beyond the ones documented in this book: our hot-air-balloon crash in Mexico, the volcano kerfuffle in Guatemala where you stood up for me against those who spewed lava at me, and in Colombia, when I got my purse stolen—your compassion helped me heal.

- Jo-e Sutton, my breast friend—sorry I nearly pulled you off the exam table with a needle in your boob! Thank you for being someone I can spew to and turn hurls into pearls. There are no words to express how grateful I am for your commitment to shadow work and your gift for alchemy in my life.

- Jewelie (Mom), Frank (Dad), my beautiful sisters, Shannon, Jeanene, Amber, and Tawni, and my nephew, Frankie, for your support and love, and all the myriad ways you help me manifest (and woman-ifest) a truly dreamy life.

- Meesha, my dreamy stepdaughter, friend, and right hand in social media and in my heart.

- My dearest besties and goddesses, Shawndara, Nancy, D'ona, Jodi, Wendi, Firestar, and Suzanne—thank you for also being the soul pillars of my life.

- Rassouli—thank you for teaching me how to OGLE and for being the best artist on planet Earth, whose Fusionart is a physical manifestation of turning the tragic into magic.

- Steve Allen (Mara Prutting and team at Steve Allen Media)—for your "miracle Monday" mentality and for believing in me all these years and for being my angel(s) in helping me get my work out into the world.

- Blyss Young, Melissa, and Ellie—thanks for sharing Claire (Claire-ity) Wineland with me and allowing me to have a personal relationship with this stunning being who continues to remind me to not take a single breath for granted.

- The Newcomer Family: Katherine, Margarita, Jay, Jason, and Jessica Janik, for sharing the amazing Brian (B-man) with me and teaching me the true meaning of the mosaic.

- Sharon Lerner for introducing me to your incredible daughter, Tess/Satya/Elsa, who's left an indelible mark on me and many others on this side of the veil.

- For my amazing neighbors, Gabriel Hacker and Jake the fireman, for helping me pull off the most amazing, crazy, and muddy photo shoot ever that has manifested in the cover of this book. Ned and Fox, for both contributing your wisdom and incredible support.

- Shannon Bradley, Timothy Courtney, Kaila Yu, and Larisa for your friendship and professional support.

- My Get-'Er-Done Authors—Corrina, Ned, Jane, Susan, Jo-e, Cole, Jewelie, Chris, Judy, Michelle, Jenni, and Ali—thank you for all that I learn about writing through your open hearts and stories.

Acknowledgments

- Aspen Matis for being the blessing of blessings, mentor of mentors, inspiring me in untold ways by your bravery, courage, and gorgeous prose.

- Sue Shapiro—if I only had a dollar for every time I quote you! Mostly for your slogan that we should *seek to live the most transparent lives possible.*

- Everyone mentioned in this book whose lives crossed with mine in a life-altering, positive way, most especially Joe Gagnon, Moira Northolt, Ron, Gregory (Billy) Keim, Jenni Murphy, Gini Gentry, Sharon Lerner, Timothy Courtney, Elias Lonsdale, Mitchel May, Dannion Brinkley, and Robert Moss, and my band of angels helping me from the other side: Tendral, Gypsy, Theresa, Nirvana, Brian, Claire, Tess/Satya/Elsa, Woofie, Shadow, Lola, and Priya.

Appendix

TRICKS, TIPS, AND HACKS
WHEN IT'S DIFFICULT TO OGLE

If you've been trying as hard as you can to OGLE but you're stuck,
try these:

Restraint of Pen and Tongue

I learned this phrase when I was steeped in the twelve steps, as I've
mentioned throughout this book. I interpret this slogan to mean
that when triggered, you should step away from doing or saying
something you might regret. In other words, avoid pressing the
send button. Once you're calm, the bees are out of your bonnet, and
you've OGLE'd the situation, if you still feel moved to press send,
then be my guest.

Take a Few Deep Breaths

According to Wim Hof, the benefits of deep breaths are overwhelm-
ingly positive not just for our physiology but for our psychology. Just
a few deep breaths can help us to transition out of the fight/flight
mode associated with our limbic brain, to our prefrontal cortex,
which allows us to take action that
reflects our more logical, rational,
civilized selves.[42]

Shake It Off

When I'm triggered, one of the best ways to get the adrenaline out of my system so I can have the clarity to OGLE is to move my body. If circumstance allows, I'll throw on my running shoes and go for a jog, take a brisk walk, or roll out my yoga matt and do a few sun salutations. If you are particularly triggered, hopefully you will have already read the "Aw, Bite Me!" story, and you'll create a private space to do what Taylor Swift and I do and shake it off!

Hurls to Pearls

My (breast) friend Jo-e and I have permission to call each other and/or leave voice memos while we're in the heat of upset. Our rule is that we don't allow ourselves to speak to the person who triggered us when we are "above a three" on a scale where one is Zen-monk calm and ten is raving-lunatic wild. Instead, we're allowed to call each other and talk out our pain (or leave a voice memo) until it transforms, naturally, into wisdom—thus, hurls to pearls. I highly suggest you make an agreement with a trusted friend (ideally who has also read this book or is familiar with OGLE) who can give you space to vent your *O* (what's Offending you) and then help guide you through the rest of the *GLE* (Good, Looking Glass, Elevate).

Play the Role of Defense Attorney

As mentioned earlier in this book, one trick that works for me is to imagine I'm a lawyer hired to represent the person who offended me. Try it. As if your life and your job depended on it, search your mind and soul for what might, possibly, in some remote corner of the universe, be good about this person's offensive behavior. At the very least, you always know that one good thing is they are highlighting one of your core values, on the opposite end of the spectrum from the defendant's behavior, that you might've taken for granted. We only know what is important to us when someone tramples it.

Be the Big One

I feel so strongly about this one that I wrote about it for my February 1 entry in my book *Luminous Humanness*:

> If somebody is acting out and not treating you with the utmost respect, tolerance, patience, and reverence, consider that they've fallen asleep and their wounded teenager has taken over. That means you, by definition, are being called to be the grown-up, to be the one with compassion so enormous that their sleepwalking doesn't ruffle you. If they were a young person, you wouldn't condemn them or join them in their nightmare. The enlightened adult wraps their spiritual arms around the young one, remembering who they truly are—a spiritual phenomenon—and whispers, "Wake up, little brother. You've fallen asleep, little sister. You're having a bad dream."

Affirmation: When others get small, I get big.[43]

If none of these tips, tricks, or hacks work, then try the golden Buddha perspective.

THE GOLDEN BUDDHA

Several hundred years ago in Thailand, Buddhist monks were forced into exile by the Burmese army. These peaceful souls were savagely beaten (some killed), their temples ransacked, sacred relics stolen, broken, and destroyed. As the ones who survived prepared to flee, carrying as many scrolls and cherished objects as they could, they realized their twenty-foot golden Buddha statue was too big and heavy to carry to safety. Several monks covered it with cement, so the invaders wouldn't realize its value and, thus, would leave it alone.

Then in 1957 a group of Thai Buddhist monks were relocating their monastery. As the monks attempted to move the giant Buddha, it slipped, causing the cement to crack. Amid the chaos and worry over having broken this great monument, one of the monks caught a glimpse of golden light emanating from the crack. With a hammer and a chisel, the monk chipped away until he revealed the statue was, in fact, made of solid gold.

The monks from hundreds of years ago had been ingenious in their strategy. The covering of the golden Buddha ensured its safety during a perilous time. This story is the perfect metaphor for what we humans do. We are all naturally golden, brighter than the light of ten thousand suns—only we forget this. We all experience some form of hardship during our domestication that causes us to cover our gold. And when our armor gets assaulted, we think this arrow to our veneer is the worst thing that could happen . . . but it turns out it can be a blessing in disguise, if we let it, because it can break us open to our golden essence.

By virtue of the fact that you are reading this now, we know your tactic way back when worked. Congratulations. You hid your gold during a difficult time, perhaps from those whose less-than-pristine intentions may have harmed, taken, or mistreated you. I'll bet, because you've been hurt, cracked open by life or by a person or by a worst-thing-that-could've-happened circumstance, you've been led to here . . . to this book . . . and to the opportunity to excavate the gold from beneath your hardened shell. Bravo! You are right on time.

Consider that this isn't a story about just your hidden gold but everyone's, so maybe now you'll see it's people's "concrete," not their "gold," that offends you. If you can be willing to don your inner archeologist (think Indiana Jones) and grab your pickax, you will discover the golden Buddha beneath the concrete.

ANOTHER POINT (OR TWO) ABOUT CONCRETE

A therapist friend of mine once said that all psychological problems stem from being overly concrete. In other words, that's when our vibration slows to such a rate that we perceive the world through the lens of black/white, good/bad, them/us. She went on to say the sign of a well-adjusted person is their ability to think symbolically, abstractly, in a way that leads them to see the world in a unified framework.

This therapist and I bonded over this concept, since one of my primary languages is dreams, which is the practice of decoding symbols, double-entendres, and wordplay to raise one's vibration. In fact, I'm fond of saying, "Metaphors be with you," and my salutation on my radio show is "Don't take your dreams . . . lying down."

To peel this onion another layer, Carl Jung taught that our souls speak to us in the language of symbol, which is the language of dreams. In other words, when we're in touch with our dreams and our dreaming mind, we're in touch with our soul. And, according to Paulo Coelho, when we are in touch with our soul, we're connected to the Soul of the World.

As I said in the previous section, we might consider that it's not the gold of the person who has offended us but their concrete outer covering that offends us. Now, take it a step further: it's only *our* concrete that gets offended and offends the people with whom we tangle. I assert that if we were brave enough and had the inner fortitude to walk through our lives with our gold on our sleeves, relating to our fellow humans gold to gold—thus, soul to soul—we would never get offended and we would never offend.

I know this is a tall order, but it's the goal, and it is, by the way, the work of our lives—perhaps the entire reason we incarnated. Even though we (as a species) have a long way to go before reaching the mountaintop, I believe that each time one of us behaves from our golden essence, we unconsciously broadcast an invitation to others, making that sacred state of being more accessible for everyone around us. And as each of us are elevated from the mud to the mountaintop, from drama to phenomena, and from the tragic to magic, may all be lifted!

Notes

DEDICATION

1. Claire's Place Foundation is a charity providing support to individuals, children, and families affected by cystic fibrosis (CF). The organization was founded by thirteen-year-old Claire Wineland, who was born with CF. For more information, please visit clairesplacefoundation.org.

INTRODUCTION

2. Jack Rosenthal, "A Terrible Thing to Waste," *New York Times Magazine*, July 31, 2009, https://www.nytimes.com/2009/08/02/magazine/02FOB -onlanguage-t.html.
3. Lorna Collier, "Growth after Trauma: Why Are Some People More Resilient Than Others—and Can It Be Taught?" *American Psychological Association* 47, no. 10 (November 2016), https://www.apa.org/monitor /2016/11/growth-trauma.
4. Claudia Wallis, "The New Science of Happiness," *Time*, January 9, 2005, https://time.com/83487/the-new-science-of-happiness/.
5. Aurora Winter, *Grief Relief in 30 Minutes: How to use the PEACE Method to Go from Heartbreak to Happiness*, (Newport, CA: Dandelion Sky Press, 2012), 1–2.
6. Eva Mozes Kor and Lisa Rojany Buccieri, *Surviving the Angel of Death: The True Story of a Mengele Twin in Auschwitz* (Terre Haute, IN: Tanglewood, 2020).

CHAPTER 1

7. "Me and Bobby McGee," lyrics by Kris Kristofferson, track 7 on Janis Joplin, *Pearl*, recorded July 27–October 4, 1970, Columbia KC 30322, 1971.
8. "Margaritaville," track 6 on Jimmy Buffet, *Changes in Latitudes, Changes in Attitudes*, recorded November 1976, ABC AB-990, 1977.

CHAPTER 2

9. Joseph Campbell and Bill Moyers, *The Power of Myth* (New York: Anchor, June 1991).

CHAPTER 3

10. Mitchell May, "Guest Speaker: Mitchell May," (lecture, Agape Spiritual Center, Beverly Hills, CA, mid-90s).

11. "The Serenity Prayer and Twelve Step Recovery," Hazelden Betty Ford Foundation, October 15, 2018, https://www.hazeldenbettyford.org /articles/the-serenity-prayer.

CHAPTER 4

12. Anne Lamott, *Bird by Bird* (New York: Anchor Books, September 2019), 218.

CHAPTER 7

13. Kelly Sullivan Walden, "No Place Like Ommmmm," in *Chicken Soup for the Soul: My Kind (of) America: 101 Stories about the True Spirit of Our Country*, ed. Amy Newmark, (Cos Cob: Chicken Soup for the Soul, 2017), 63–70.
14. "History: Estonia's 5,000+ Year Journey," The Singing Revolution, accessed February 2016, https://singingrevolution.com/about/history.

CHAPTER 8

15. A version of "The Burning Bougainvillea" was published in *EVOLVE!* magazine: Kelly Sullivan Walden, "Earned Optimism & the Burning Bougainvillea," *EVOLVE!* 20, no. 2 (Fall 2021), 11.
16. A. Justin Sterling, "Sterling Women's Weekend," (Los Angeles, CA, 1998), https://sterling-institute.com/womens-weekend.

CHAPTER 9

17. The "Tendral" story was published in Kelly Sullivan Walden, "Introduction," in *Dia de los Muertos Oracle Deck* (Victoria, Australia: Blue Angel, 2022), 1.
18. A medicine wheel is a circular rock formation with an altar in the center dedicated to the seven directions: east, south, west, north, above, below, and within.
19. Viktor E. Frankl, *Man's Search for Meaning: The Classic Tribute to Hope from the Holocaust* (New York: Pocket Books, 1985), 130–131.
20. Viktor Frankl Institut, "Interview with Dr. Viktor Frankl part I," YouTube, video, 8:41, posted by "yecto," 2007, https://www.youtube.com /watch?v=9EIxGrIc_6g.
21. My team and I gratefully partnered with TECHO in the building of ten homes: https://techo.org/.

CHAPTER 10

22. Elisabeth Kübler-Ross, *On Death and Dying: What the Dying Have to Teach Doctors, Nurses, Clergy & Their Own Families* (New York: The Macmillan Company, 1969).
23. *The Social Dilemma*, directed by Jeff Orlowski, written by Vickie Curtis, Davis Coombe, and Jeff Orlowski (Netflix, 2020), https://www.netflix .com/title/81254224.

CHAPTER 11

24. Kelly Sullivan Walden, "November 16th: You Are De-Light," in *Luminous Humanness: 365 Ways to Go, Grow & Glow to Make It Your Best Year Yet* (Woodbury: Llewellyn Publications, 2021), 355.

25. Judy Bloom, *Are You There, God? It's Me, Margaret* (New York: Bradbury Press, 1970).

CHAPTER 12

26. Dannion Brinkley, personal communication with author, September 2008.

CHAPTER 14

27. Judy Wilkens-Smith, interview by Kelly Sullivan Walden, "Episode 2: Searching for Satya, the Girl with the Blue Ukulele," June 27, 2021, in *Ask Doctor Dream* (now *The Kelly Sullivan Walden Show*), produced by Unity Online Radio (now www.MindBodySpirit.FM), podcast, audio, 21:57–22:31, https://megaphonelink/UOR1770366787.

28. Timothy Courtney, interview by Kelly Sullivan Walden, "Episode 7: Palm Springs Psychic Medium Timothy Courtney," September 1, 2021, in *Ask Doctor Dream* (now *The Kelly Sullivan Walden Show*), produced by Unity Online Radio (now www.MindBodySpirit.FM), podcast, audio, https://megaphone.link/UOR1188046097.

29. Elias Lonsdale, interview by Kelly Sullivan Walden, "Episode 8: Finding Magic in the Tragic: The Dream Conclusion," September 8, 2021, in *Ask Doctor Dream* (now *The Kelly Sullivan Walden Show*), produced by Unity Online Radio (now www.MindBodySpirit.FM), podcast, audio, 20:29–22:31, https://megaphone.link/UOR1386904156.

CHAPTER 15

30. Kelly Sullivan Walden, "Mosaic," in *Chicken Soup for the Soul: Dreams and Premonitions: 101 Amazing Stories of Miracles, Divine Intervention, and Insight*, ed. Amy Newmark (Cos Cob: Chicken Soup for the Soul, 2015), 11–14.

31. Jay Newcomer, email message to author, November 2011.

CHAPTER 16

32. The Claire's Place Foundation, https://clairesplacefoundation.org/.

CHAPTER 17

33. Shel Silverstein, "The Voice," in *Falling Up* (New York: HarperCollins, 2006), 38.

CHAPTER 18

34. Karen Stollznow, "Why Women Don't Immediately Report Sexual Assault," *Psychology Today*, December 21, 2021, https://www .psychologytoday.com/us/blog/speaking-in-tongues/202112 /why-women-dont-immediately-report-sexual-assault.

CHAPTER 19

35. Joseph Campbell, *The Hero with a Thousand Faces: The Collected Works of Joseph Campbell* (Novato, CA: New World Library, July 28, 2008), 90.

CHAPTER 21

36. Professor Susan Shapiro, personal communication with author, September 2019.

CHAPTER 23

37. Marshall Rosenberg, "Nonviolent Communication," Agape Spiritual Center, Los Angeles, CA, 2006).

CHAPTER 25

38. Kelly Sullivan Walden, "February 9th, As They Are Lifted, You Are Lifted," in *Luminous Humanness: 365 Ways to Go, Grow & Glow to Make It Your Best Year Yet* (Woodbury: Llewellyn Publications, 2021), 60.

CHAPTER 27

39. Kelly Sullivan Walden, "Card 25: Whale of a Time," in *Hero's Journey Dream Oracle Deck* (Woodbury: Llewellyn Publications, 2019), 90.

CHAPTER 28

40. For more information on Laurel Canyon Animal Company, please visit laurelcanyonanimalcompany.com.

41. "Take Charge of Your Health," Caroline Myss, accessed April 26, 2022, https://www.myss.com/free-resources/take-charge/take-charge-of -your-health/.

APPENDIX

42. Wim Hof, "Wim Hof Method Breathing," Wim Hof Method, accessed April 26, 2022, https://www.wimhofmethod.com/breathing-exercises.

43. Kelly Sullivan Walden, "February 1: Be the Big One," in *Luminous Humanness: 365 Ways to Go, Grow & Glow to Make It Your Best Year Yet* (Woodbury: Llewellyn Publications, 2021), 52.

About The Author

Kelly Sullivan Walden is an international bestselling author of ten books, four oracle decks, two journals, and two apps: The Hero's Journey Dream Oracle and Luminous Humanness Meditations. She's an award-winning dream expert and an interfaith minister with a Doctor of Ministry degree. Additionally, she's a certified clinical hypnotherapist, practitioner of religious science, inspirational speaker, and workshop facilitator. Kelly is known as Doctor Dream; her unique approach to dream therapy led her to become a trusted advisor, coach, and consultant, enriching the lives of thousands of individuals across the globe, from Fortune 500 executives to celebrities to stay-at-home parents. Her career in dream therapy led her to create and host the *Kelly Sullivan Walden Show* (aka Doctor Dream) podcast as well as to found DreamWork Practitioner Training, an online program that teaches people to develop dream mastery. Kelly earned her master's and doctorate in ministry from The New Seminary in New York, the oldest interfaith seminary in the world. Together with her husband, Dana, Kelly cofounded the Dream Project and CHIME IN: youth-empowerment initiatives that support the United Nations Sustainable Development Goals. For more information and a free dreamtime meditation to enhance dream recall, please visit KellySullivanWalden.com.